Women in Medieval English Society

Written primarily for undergraduates, this book judiciously weighs the evidence for and against the various theories relating to the position of women at different time periods. Professor Mate examines the evidence relating to the major issues deciding the position of women in medieval English society, and asks questions such as, did women enjoy a rough equality in the Anglo-Saxon period that they subsequently lost? Did queens at certain periods exercise real political clout or was their power limited to questions of patronage? Did women's participation in the economy grant them considerable independence and allow them to postpone or delay marriage? Professor Mate also demonstrates that class as well as gender was very important in determining age at marriage and opportunities for power and influence. Although some women at some time periods did make short-term gains, Professor Mate challenges the dominant view that major transformations in women's position occurred in the century after the Black Death.

MAVIS E. MATE is Professor of Medieval History at the University of Oregon. She has written many articles for major journals and is the author of *Daughters, Wives and Widows after the Black Death: Women in Sussex 1350–1530* (1998).

New Studies in Economic and Social History

Edited for the Economic History Society by
Michael Sanderson
University of East Anglia, Norwich

This series, specially commissioned by the Economic History Society, provides a guide to the current interpretations of the key themes of economic and social history in which advances have recently been made or in which there has been significant debate.

In recent times economic and social history has been one of the most flourishing areas of historical study. This has mirrored the increasing relevance of the economic and social sciences both in a student's choice of career and in forming a society at large more aware of the importance of these issues in their everyday lives. Moreover specialist interests in business, agricultural and welfare history, for example, have themselves burgeoned and there has been an increased interest in the economic development of the wider world. Stimulating as these scholarly developments have been for the specialist, the rapid advance of the subject and the quantity of new publications make it difficult for the reader to gain an overview of particular topics, let alone the whole field.

New Studies in Economic and Social History is intended for students and their teachers. It is designed to introduce them to fresh topics and to enable them to keep abreast of recent writing and debates. All the books in the series are written by a recognized authority in the subject, and the arguments and issues are set out in a critical but unpartisan fashion. The aim of the series is to survey the current state of scholarship, rather than to provide a set of pre-packaged conclusions.

The series had been edited since its inception in 1968 by Professors M. W. Flinn, T. C. Smout and L. A. Clarkson, and is currently edited by Dr Michael Sanderson. From 1968 it was published by Macmillan as *Studies in Economic History*, and after 1974 as *Studies in Economic and Social History*. From 1995 *New Studies in Economic and Social History* is being published on behalf of the Economic History Society by Cambridge University Press. This new series includes some of the titles previously published by Macmillan as well as new titles, and reflects the ongoing development throughout the world of this rich seam of history.

For a full list of titles in print, please see the end of the book.

Women in Medieval English Society

Prepared for the Economic History Society by

Mavis E. Mate
University of Oregon

PUBLISHED BY THE PRESS SYNDICATE OF THE UNIVERSITY OF CAMBRIDGE
The Pitt Building, Trumpington Street, Cambridge CB2 1RP, United Kingdom

CAMBRIDGE UNIVERSITY PRESS
The Edinburgh Building, Cambridge, CB2 2RU, UK   http://www.cup.cam.ac.uk
40 West 20th Street, New York, NY 10011–4211, USA   http://www.cup.org
10 Stamford Road, Oakleigh, Melbourne 3166, Australia

First published 1999

Printed in the United Kingdom at the University Press, Cambridge

Typeset in 10/12$\frac{1}{2}$ pt Plantin   [CE]

A catalogue record for this book is available from the British Library

Library of Congress cataloguing in publication data
Mate, Mavis E., 1933–
Women in medieval English society / prepared for the Economic History Society by Mavis E. Mate.
        p.   cm. – (New studies in economic and social history)
Includes bibliographical references (p.   ) and index.
ISBN 0 521 58322 5 (hardback). – ISBN 0 521 58733 6 (paperback)
1. Women – England – History – Middle Ages, 500–1500.
2. Women – England – Social conditions.
3. Women – England – Economic conditions.
4. Social history – Medieval, 500–1500.
I. Economic History Society.   II. Title.   III. Series.
HQ1599.E5M38   1999
305.42′0942′0902 – dc21   98–43628   CIP

ISBN 0 521 58322 5 hardback
ISBN 0 521 58733 6 paperback

Contents

1
Introduction

More has been written about medieval women in the last fifteen years than in the previous one hundred and fifty. Female authors, like the Frenchwoman Christine de Pisan, and the Englishwomen Julian of Norwich and Margery Kempe, have been re-discovered and new editions and translations of their works have been produced. Queens are no longer seen as mere appendages of their husbands and have merited their own biographies. Tax records and manorial court-rolls have revealed the names of thousands of women while fascinating human insights can be gained from women's wills and letters. Yet administrative records, whether those of the central government or local manorial accounts were compiled for financial and jurisdictional reasons and the women who appear in them represent just a small fraction of the total female population. Thus historians know a great deal more about widows who held property and who enjoyed legal autonomy than they know about wives whose legal identity was subsumed within that of their husbands. So, too, much more is known about women as ale-brewers, because for much of the Middle Ages brewers were regularly fined, but much less is known about women's work as laundresses and seamstresses, since they were never formally regulated. Any record, read in isolation, gives but one facet of the total picture. Wills, written by women, reveal fascinating insights about female piety and personal relationships towards the end of life, but say nothing about their attitudes and situation at other points in their life-cycle.

With the vast explosion in the material dealing with medieval women's history and the imperfections of many of the sources, considerable debate has arisen about the position of women. Is gender, for example, more important than class? Gender determines that wives were primarily responsible for household management and child-care and that this work, precisely because it was women's work, was less highly regarded than the work carried out by men. Women, of all social classes, were depicted not only as weaker physically, but weaker rationally and morally. Women generally had a more restricted choice of occupation, and fewer opportunities for education and the acquisition of property than males in their social group. On the other hand, the material well-being of women was clearly determined by their social class. Housing, diet and clothing all varied significantly across the social scale. Furthermore, although aristocratic women enjoyed fewer rights than their brothers, they had far greater access to education, property and political power than did any peasant woman.

The opportunities available to a woman varied not only according to her social class, but also to the stage that she had reached in her life-cycle. Daughters, whatever their rank in society, were legally under the control and authority of their fathers. Wives were also subjected to the power and authority of their husbands. Generally only widows had any measure of legal autonomy. Examples of power and independence wielded by wealthy, aristocratic, widows cannot be extrapolated into a high status enjoyed by all women in that society or indeed for all women in that social class. So too a woman might enjoy more or less *de facto* freedom according to the different stages of her life. By the fourteenth and fifteenth centuries the daughters of labourers and artisans frequently left home at the age of twelve or thirteen to work for others as servants. Away from direct parental control, they were freer to chose their own marriage partner than a young aristocratic girl whose parents saw her marriage as a means to consolidate their property or expand their network of allies. Wives, in both countryside and town, who supplemented the family income through brewing, spinning or the sale of produce, could sometimes spend their earnings as they wished, despite their husbands' legal authority. Yet the same women as widows might choose or be required to live with a married son or daughter, thus relinquishing some of their former independence. So, in talking about women, it is important to distinguish both what social class is being discussed and whether the women concerned were daughters, wives or widows. The legal autonomy that widowhood brought was of little value if the widow herself had few, if any, resources at her disposal.

One reason for debate is that historians use different criteria to assess women's power, authority and status. For some, legal rights – the ability to make a will and to control and alienate land – is the most important factor: for others what matters is economic power – the ability to participate in the workforce and to contribute to the family income. Even more significant, perhaps, is the lens through which women are viewed. Those historians who are aware of the power of patriarchy and the limitations that it imposes on women tend to stress what women cannot do, whereas historians who emphasize women as capable and independent beings, able to cope with difficult circumstances, stress what rights and opportunities women did enjoy. Thus, whereas the first group tend to see the glass as half empty, the second group see it as half full.

Regional variation in economic development and legal custom also had a profound influence on women's lives throughout the Middle Ages. Taking care of animals, and above all work in the dairy, was always seen as suitable employment for women, but the opportunities for women to work outside the home for extended periods were obviously greater in pastoral than arable areas. Likewise, widows might have an easier time managing on their own if they could engage in pastoral husbandry which was not labour intensive. On the other hand, women were expected to help with the harvest on their own land, if not for others. In arable areas in particular the late summer months were extremely busy times for women as they juggled family and household demands with agricultural tasks.

In the century following the Norman Conquest the rules under which freeholders held their land became well defined and common to the whole country. In contrast, land held 'at the will of the lord' was subject to a bewildering variety of customs. Over much of the country, customary land followed the same practices as freehold land and went to the eldest son, but in some places land was either inherited by the youngest son, or divided equally among all sons. Provisions for widows ranged from half the holding until the heir came of age to the whole holding for life, irrespective of any remarriage. In some places tenants had the right to sell the odd acre or half acre as family circumstances changed, whereas elsewhere lords insisted that any alienation had to be in the form of the entire holding. Such customs affected family structure and kinship ties as well as economic well-being. Life for women in the west Midlands was not identical with that for women in East Anglia.

Sources are more abundant for one class at one time period and another class at another time. This makes comparisons across classes and across centuries difficult. None the less, some historians do believe that Anglo-Saxon women enjoyed more rights than their Anglo-Norman successors. Indeed, the Anglo-Saxon period has been portrayed as a kind of 'golden age' in which men and women lived on terms of rough equality. Other historians, while accepting the notion that women enjoyed greater opportunities at one time than another, place the 'golden age' in the later Middle Ages, when, after the population losses of the Black Death, women were recruited into the labour force in large numbers. The debate on Anglo-Saxon versus Anglo-Norman women, however, focuses almost exclusively on the nobility, since the sources are not available for women in other social classes. In contrast, the discussion on the late medieval golden age revolves around the position of peasant and urban women. The whole notion of a golden age, moreover, has been challenged by historians such as Pauline Stafford and Judith Bennett who stress the continuities across time.

In the following pages I shall look at the ways in which historians have seen the position of women in medieval society from the beginning of the Anglo-Saxon period to the end of the fifteenth century within two broadly defined time periods. Within each the discussion will centre on the legal rights enjoyed by women, their contribution to the economy, and their political and religious power, such as influence wielded by queens and abbesses. Attention will also be given to discussions about the existence or otherwise of a 'golden age' and to changes over time, since these are questions that have sparked considerable debate.

2
Early medieval society
(*c.* 600 to 1250)

The view that Anglo-Saxon women enjoyed rights and privileges that they subsequently lost at the time of the Norman Conquest has a long history. In the 1890s the American historian Florence Buckstaff pointed to the deterioration of women's legal position with the introduction of Norman, feudal law (Buckstaff, 1893). In the 1950s, in her influential book *The English Woman in History*, Doris Mary Stenton stressed the 'rough equality' that Anglo-Saxon women enjoyed with men, but added that this partnership was subsequently ended with the imposition of a Norman, military, society (Stenton, 1957: 28, 348). In the 1960s and 1970s when the new study of women's history began to take hold, female historians were delighted to find examples of powerful, independent women to set alongside the stories of male leaders that had dominated so much historical writing. Stenton's insistence on the rough equality of Anglo-Saxon women was picked up and repeated together with the view of the negative impact of the Norman Conquest. Historians such as Sheila Dietrich, in her introductory survey of women in Anglo-Saxon society, emphasized their control over property and the active and respected role of abbesses and missionaries in the church. Although denying that it was a golden age for women, Dietrich does suggest that future research into the period might produce examples of 'women's influence and freedom of action that would make aspects of even the twentieth century appear dark' (Dietrich, 1979: 44).

Religious and political life

Did Anglo-Saxon women have influence on public affairs? They were evidently not lost in their husbands' public identity. The women themselves remained responsible for their own crimes and actions, and marriage did not end the obligation of a woman's natal kin to help her in the payment of compensation. Women regularly appeared in recorded legal disputes, although only as defendants and, when a case involved a woman, other women might act as oath-helpers. On the other hand no Anglo-Saxon woman received royal office as reeve or ealdorman. The only women who held any kind of administrative positions were those who had been to some extent degendered. Abbesses and female religious, by their virginity and the abandonment of the female reproductive role, had become more like men. Above all, the queen in her capacity as king's spouse could fill a special role. After the early tenth century she alone might be listed among witnesses to royal charters (Stafford, 1989). None the less, both abbesses and queens operated within and accepted the norms of a patriarchal society, in which the activities of males were accorded more value than the activities of women. Thus abbesses served a male God and never questioned their inability to become priests, and queens used what power they had to further the careers of their sons, not their daughters. Yet if one accepts the definition of power put forward by Pauline Stafford – the ability to act effectively, to take part in events with some chance of success – then both abbesses and queens exercised power (Stafford, 1997: 11).

Historians who believe in the equality and high status of Anglo-Saxon women point to the prestige and influence of abbesses in the seventh-century double monasteries, which housed communities of both men and women. Female religious participated in theological debates, church synods and missionary activity. Lady Stenton, writing of Abbess Hild of Whitby, states 'Few English women have ever exercised a more far-reaching influence on the world they knew' (Stenton, 1957: 13). The major source for Hild's life – Bede's *Ecclesiastical History* – in fact under-represented her contribution. In Bede's account of the synod that was held at Whitby to determine on what date to celebrate Easter, Hild herself was not seen or heard. So, too, Bede mentions that her monastery produced five future bishops of the Anglo-Saxon church, but says nothing about her learning, or whether she or other nuns taught the future bishops, or whether they educated other women who went on to become abbesses elsewhere (Hollis, 1992: 243–70). Hild, however, is credited with recognizing the poetic talent of Caedmon, converting him to the monastic life and encouraging him to write religious, vernacular verse. Yet, as has been pointed out, in appropriating Caedmon's poetic talent in the service of patriarchal Christianity, Hild was also reproducing patriarchy (Lees and Overing, 1994: 45). Hild and other abbesses, such as her niece Aelffled, were able to exercise such influence as they did partly because of their office and partly because of their wealth and birth, especially their association with one of the royal houses. Christian office was enhanced by the fact of royal origins and although they sometimes witnessed charters as abbesses, they also did so as members of the royal family (Stafford, 1997: 15). Their lives tell us nothing about the influence and opportunities for non-aristocratic women.

None the less, for a brief period, at a time when very few people, either male or female, were literate, some noblewomen were able to receive an academic, literary education comparable to that of male religious. Excavations of the monastery of Whitby and other sites have uncovered plentiful evidence of busy *scriptoria* where the nuns would have copied manuscripts. Aldhelm's treatise, *On Virginity*, written at the request of the nuns of Barking, indicates that they studied the scriptures, exegetical commentaries and grammar, together with 'old stories of the historians and entries of the chroniclers' (Leyser, 1995: 19–39; Hollis, 1992: 75–111). This work, like that of the early correspondence of the missionary Boniface, attests to the respect that men within the church had for the learning and activities of these nuns. In the seventh century the church within the various English kingdoms had no organized, parochial or educational structure. Female houses, like male houses, were able to become the focus of religious and social activity for their regions. They aided in the work of conversion; their schools served both men and women and they were responsible for the pastoral care of the whole area, including the giving of help and advice to ordinary lay men and women. Even though

Archbishop Theodore, who came to Canterbury in 669, openly disapproved of double monasteries, he had little option but to tolerate them. It was not until after the Viking invasions had destroyed a considerable number of female houses (including double foundations) that their pastoral responsibilities were taken over by episcopal minsters (Schulenburg, 1989).

Although royal and aristocratic women were active supporters of the movement for monastic reform that began in the tenth century, female institutions outside Wessex did not recover their former influence. In their zeal for clerical celibacy, the reformers eschewed all contact with women. The double houses for women and men disappeared and women were confined to single-sexed houses that were strictly cloistered. Far more land was given to refounded male institutions than female ones. Nunneries in Kent that had flourished in the heyday of the Kentish monarchy found little support under the rule of powerful West Saxon kings. After the Viking invasions their lands were absorbed back into the West Saxon royal fisc and so were not available for the establishment of new convents (Yorke, 1989). When, in the 970s the task of protecting and patronizing English nunneries was given to the queen, female houses became dependent on the interests and ambition of individual queens. Under Aelfthryth (the wife of Edgar and the mother of Aethelred II) some monasteries suffered, as she used royal patronage to increase her own power and influence. She dislodged the abbess of Barking, for example, in order to control its strategic estates along the Thames. On the other hand she did use some of the land she had obtained by virtue of her status as queen to found two major new nunneries at Amesbury and Wherwell. At neither the new foundations nor the older houses did conventual learning attain the earlier levels of scholarship. However, continued grants of land to the six West Saxon nunneries made them far wealthier than other surviving nunneries and in 1066 they held estates in fourteen shires. Two of them – Shaftesbury and Wilton – were among the richest monastic houses in England (Meyer, 1991; Halpin, 1994). Their abbesses not only managed the internal affairs of the houses, but on their vast estates controlled the affairs of dependent tenants.

During the eleventh century male and female aristocratic donors primarily gave their land and money to male communities or recently established parish churches rather than to women's houses (Meyer, 1977; Schulenburg 1989). Thus, outside of Wessex, nunneries were poorly endowed, or, in the north of England, virtually non-existent. Why did this decline occur? Schulenburg points to a new atmosphere of 'heightened fear and suspicion of female sexuality' in the wake of the reform movement (Schulenburg, 1989: 239). But other factors were clearly at work. Donors were generally hoping to reap some spiritual benefits for their gifts. Women could not celebrate mass, whereas secular canons and monks who were also priests, could offer perpetual intercessory prayers for the benefit of the souls of donors. So too an eleventh-century parish or manorial church brought its proprietors substantial financial advantages. It could be sold or bequeathed and the patrons retained advowson – the right to appoint the church's priests – and part of the revenues coming from oblations and dues such as tithes. Such churches became centres for familial devotion and burial and allowed female benefactors an opportunity to influence local affairs in ways not otherwise open to them (Halpin, 1994).

Furthermore, despite the overall contraction in the number of female institutions, religious life for women did continue to thrive in the late tenth and eleventh centuries, albeit in a less regular guise. Widows who wanted to lead a religious life, but who may have been reluctant to submit to the authority of an abbess, affiliated in some informal way with a nearby male foundation and lived either as independent anchoresses or with a small group of other like-minded women, often on their own estates. Their lifestyle did not differ greatly from that of later, better-known anchoresses such as the early twelfth-century recluse, Christina of Markyate. Patricia Halpin, therefore, sees considerable continuity in women's religious life in pre- and post-Conquest England (Halpin, 1994). No major change occurred until the mid-twelfth century, when both the number and variety of female houses multiplied dramatically. Small groups of women who had been surviving as nuns in ruined priories, old cells or poorly endowed churches, were provided with additional land and resources so that a priory could be established. In addition, laymen founded totally new houses: Gilbert of Sempringham was responsible for nine new monasteries and Premonstratensian canons aided the

foundation of three houses for women. Finally, laypeople established Cistercian houses. Although these houses were not fully
incorporated into the Cistercian order, the women adopted Cistercian customs, used Cistercian missals, and dressed in habits of a
Cistercian type. In 1130, in all of England, there were about
twenty religious communities for women: in 1165 England had
more than a hundred houses, nearly half of them springing up in
the north of England where women had had few options for a
religious life. Approximately a quarter of these new foundations
were actually for women and men. Gilbertine monasteries, for
example, included not only nuns and lay sisters, but canons and
lay brothers. Few of the nuns who joined the new foundations
came from either royal or noble families and abbesses were
generally willing to accept control exercised by the canons and
monks. Not one of the new abbesses enjoyed the same independence as her seventh-century predecessors. On the other hand, by
the end of the twelfth century women from a much broader social
spectrum did have the opportunity to choose a religious life.

In contrast to the position of the powerful abbess, seventh- and
eighth-century queens did not have a recognized role. That situation changed in the tenth century as queens acquired a significant
landed estate both from their own kinsmen and from the king. In
addition, the practice of serial monogamy meant that the rules of
succession to the crown were not clear-cut. Sons by successive
wives and concubines formed a group of throne-worthy males who
competed with each other. A dowager queen who did her utmost
to advance her son at the expense of his half-brothers might reap
her reward if her son did become king. Her position as 'mother of
the king' was further strengthened if she had powerful kinsmen
who could throw their support behind the young monarch.
Finally, the anointing of Edgar's wife, Aelfthryth, in 973 gave her,
and all subsequent anointed queens, a new status as a consecrated
person. A queen during her lifetime might thus fill many roles,
either consecutively or concurrently. She was a consecrated and
crowned wife, an anointed queen, and, on the death of her
husband, the mother of the next king, but she was also *conlaterana
regis* – the person who stands beside and aids the king (Stafford,
1997a; 1997b).

The influence of any queen, however, was very dependent on the support of her husband or her son and could disappear as circumstances altered. In the early eleventh century, after Emma, the daughter of the Duke of Normandy, married the Danish ruler, Cnut, she was able to capitalize on her role as peace-weaver between English, Norman and Dane. Her patronage paralleled that of her husband and she gained support with her gifts of textiles, precious metalwork and relics. Her influence was sought and acknowledged in a range of transactions from land purchases, and the confirmation of episcopal appointments, to the making of wills. On Cnut's death she seized the royal treasury and seems to have taken control of Cnut's mercenary forces in her struggle to secure the throne for one of her sons. The accession of Harthacanute (her son by Cnut) saw her influence peak. But, after his early death, and the granting of the crown to Edward the Confessor (her son by her first husband, Aethelred), Emma lost everything, not only influence but much of her wealth and land as well (Stafford, 1989; 1997b).

Eleventh-century queens exercised power partly through their office but partly as a result of their control over their own household and over vast landed estates. Emma, until the loss of her power in 1043, was the richest woman in England. Her daughter-in-law Edith (the wife of Edward the Confessor) was the richest woman in 1066. The lands assigned to her in Domesday were worth between £1,570 and £2,000 per annum and included towns and their revenues, as well as churches and religious communities and the profits of justice (Stafford, 1997b: 123). Likewise both Matilda and Maud, the wives respectively of both William the Conqueror and Henry I, had been able to enter the lands assigned for their dower during their lifetimes. Not only did they have control over tenants who might be great lords, but they could use these resources in support of patronage and their households. Service in the queen's household became a useful springboard for subsequent episcopal office. Yet by the end of Henry I's reign queenly power was being eroded as professional administrators began to take over some of the tasks of government. Maud, who early in her husband's reign participated in meetings of the king's court, had less opportunity to wield public authority. What was left was the role of intercessor. Lois Honeycott has shown how

Maud consciously adapted her behaviour towards the pattern presented in the didactic literature that she read, but at the same time sought to shape and manipulate the ideal to her advantage (Honeycott, 1995). None the less, such influence as she wielded had now become indirect rather than direct.

In a military society which valued courage in the heat of battle, women were at a distinct disadvantage since they were not trained to fight. The defence of a castle, or subsequently a manor house, in the absence of the lord, was an acceptable role for women throughout the Middle Ages, but active participation in military manoeuvres was not. Queens such as Emma and Edith regularly held and defended fortified places that formed part of their landed endowment. Aethelflaed, who ruled Mercia from 911 to 918 after the death of her husband, successfully engaged in the siege and defence of towns, castles and fortified places, but she did not lead troops in battle (Stafford, 1983: 118). Similarly, Matilda, the daughter of Henry I, when she was fighting against Stephen for her inheritance in England, participated in sieges that led her into danger, but was quite unable to conduct the kind of 'dashing campaign' that her son Henry II was later to employ (Chibnall, 1991: 97). As a result, despite the capture of Stephen in 1141, Matilda was not able to make good her claim to rule the whole of England. None the less, for the eight and a half years she remained within the country, she issued charters in her own name, received vassals and had her own coins struck at Bristol and Cardiff. Despite the general reluctance to accept a woman as ruler, she maintained the support of a handful of magnates and bishops and was never driven out of her heartland. She exercised power directly, not through the intermediary of a husband or son, and reaped the consequences of her mistakes in judgement. But without experience in military affairs the best that she could do was to transfer her inheritance to her son.

The life of Henry II's queen, Eleanor of Aquitaine, illustrates well how much royal women were affected by external circumstances and the personalities of the males in their families. Assessments of her power depend on which part of her life is being discussed. Honeycott and Parsons emphasize that as queen she did not enter into her dower lands until after the death of Henry II, so she had no independent source of income within England.

They also point out that Eleanor ceased to witness royal charters after 1155 and to issue writs in her own name after 1163. Furthermore, after she encouraged her sons in their rebellion against their father, Henry was able to keep her under strict surveillance in England during the last years of his life (Honeycott, 1995; Parsons, 1995a and b). In contrast, Elizabeth Brown emphasizes Eleanor's impressive achievements as regent of England before 1163 and as its ruler during much of her son Richard's reign. Eleanor arranged and perhaps personally negotiated the marriage of Richard and Berengaria, the daughter of the Queen of Navarre. After Richard was captured by the emperor on his return home from the East, Eleanor acted as judge, dispenser of grace and favour, and as supervisor of the country's defences, while working unceasingly to secure his release. Brown concludes that to the end of her life Eleanor remained 'intoxicated' with the exercise of power and political manoeuvring, at which she excelled. Yet Brown does recognize that after 1163 Henry II firmly controlled the decisions that were made, allowing her to exercise authority in her duchy of Aquitaine when it suited him and taking that authority away after the rising of his sons in 1173 (Brown, 1976). As with so many women of this time, it was the absence of their menfolk that gave them the opportunity to exercise public power.

Women in the economy

Female as well as male slaves existed in late Anglo-Saxon England. Precise numbers are impossible to determine, but it has been estimated that in 1086, at the time of the Domesday inquest, there were around 33,000 male slaves (roughly 12 per cent of the total estimated population), many of whom would have been married. In addition, a further 706 female slaves (*ancillae*) are recorded. These are obviously not the only such slaves in existence, but seem to have been women holding positions of responsibility on an estate (Moore, 1989; Pelteret, 1995: 202–3). Some clearly worked as dairy-maids. Others were probably domestic servants, engaged in household tasks or in productive work like weaving. In the tenth century, for example, a widow, Wynflaed, in her will bequeathed to her grand-daughter two female slaves – *ane crencestre* and *ane semestre* – the former some kind of weaver, although the precise meaning is not clear, and the latter a woman with sewing and embroidery skills (Stenton, 1957; Fell, 1984: 49; Jewell, 1996: 35). Wynflaed cannot have been the only wealthy noblewoman to have used female slaves in these tasks. The *ancillae* were expected to work all day for at least six days a week and sometimes they worked at least part of the day on Sunday as well.

Married women, whatever their social class, contributed by their labour to the economic well-being of their families. The regular presence in Anglo-Saxon female graves of thread boxes, spindle whorls and weaving batons suggest a public identification of women with the role of cloth producer. Likewise, the existence of cooking vessels illustrates their pivotal role in feeding their families. Moreover, by the Viking age grave-goods such as small sickles show that women were also involved in outdoor work on the farm, especially at the time of the harvest (Jesch, 1991: 10–22). The existence of masculine and feminine nouns for bakers and brewers also suggests that women were involved in both trades. In most cases this work fed and clothed their own families and helped to maintain their land, but was unpaid.

A few women, however, worked for some kind of commercial compensation. In Domesday is the oft-quoted reference to Leof-geat, who, 'in 1086 as in 1066 did gold embroidery for the king and queen'. She held land from the king, but it is not clear whether she received any other reward. Domesday also records that in Chester both men and women brewed ale and could be placed on the dungstool if they brewed it badly. This surely hints at production for sale (Stafford, 1989: 82; Fell, 1984: 49). Similarly, in the countryside women were paid for their work in the dairy. In the tract *Rectitudines*, a text from the early eleventh century that specifies the rights and duties of estate workers, there is a reference to a woman who makes cheese and butter for the lord's table and who is paid in kind with a grant of cheeses and butter-milk (Fell, 1984: 47; Jewell, 1996: 35).

When manorial and urban records become available in the twelfth and thirteenth centuries it is clear that both brewing and work in the dairy – milking cows and ewes and making cheese and butter – were regarded as women's work. Brewsters in both town and countryside were subject to regulation and if they brewed weak and insufficient ale might have to forfeit their brew. Dairy-maids could be hired for just the summer and the autumn, but if they were hired for the whole year could receive the same money wage as male workers on the estate, but a lower payment of grain. On the manor of Combe, belonging to the abbey of Bec, the ploughman received one quarter of grain every ten weeks when he was not being fed at the lord's table, whereas the dairy-maid received one quarter every sixteen weeks in the winter and one quarter every twelve weeks in the summer (Chibnall, 1951). Other women can be found working in the kitchen, and making wicks for candles in the bakery and brewhouse of St Mary's, Worcester (Hale, 1865) and a few women are identified as weavers and laundresses. Similarly, within early towns such as Leicester, women can be found baking, brewing, selling fish and preparing wool. One widow, Matilda Cagge, carried on her husband's business as a vintner. No tradeswoman at Leicester, however, was ever admitted to the guild (Bateson, 1899). In some other towns such as Andover the right to membership in the guild merchant could be inherited by females as well as males. Daughters, and occasionally sisters, can be found entering the guild 'by right of inheritance'. They often transferred their right, however, to a son or husband (Gross, 1890).

Women could also inherit or be given land. In most cases, so long as they were married, the land was managed and controlled by their husbands. Unmarried women – both young women and widows – could spend their revenues as they pleased, but widows usually enjoyed only a life interest and could not alienate their property. None the less, if they kept the land and buildings in good shape until such time as the heirs took over, they performed a useful service. Moreover, whenever land was held from a lord for a certain amount of labour services, the female tenant, like her male counterpart, was responsible for those services. She could either hire male labour or carry them out herself. On the manor of Ogbourne St George, in the mid-thirteenth century, nine female cottagers were expected to weed, raise hay and stack and reap. And in the manor of Combe two female tenants, each holding an acre of land, were responsible for washing and shearing sheep, reaping in the autumn and carrying small goods such as hens (Chibnall, 1951).

In the twelfth and early thirteenth centuries women, as in Anglo-Saxon times, carried out a great deal of unpaid labour around the house and in the fields. In addition to meal preparation, child-care and laundry, they brewed and spun for family consumption. In the countryside they took care of the family's cows, pigs and poultry as well as the crops growing in the garden. After the harvest was over, it was often women who had the right and privilege of gleaning. Moreover, in some places both unmarried daughters and wives were expected to help bring in the lord's harvest; elsewhere wives were excused (Hale, 1865). Within the towns wives helped their husbands carry out his craft and/or sold goods in his shop. In Leicester the wives of butchers were specifically granted permission to sell cooked meat (Bateson, 1899). Finally women contributed to the family's food supply by gathering goods such as fruit, nuts or shell-fish, depending on the resources of their immediate neighbourhood.

The legal rights of women

The significance of the Norman Conquest in reducing women's legal position was challenged by Anne Klinck (1982), who insisted that greater changes occurred within the Anglo-Saxon period than in the period immediately before and after 1066. The early law codes dealing with sexual offences, such as the squeezing of an arm, as well as with the violation and abduction of women, were regarded by Lady Stenton as protecting women from violence and safeguarding their honour (Stenton, 1957: 9). To Klinck, however, they proved that in the seventh and eighth centuries women were under the guardianship of men. The fines paid by offenders went to the male guardians (or owners in the case of slaves), not to the women themselves, and marriage was regarded as a purchase. In the law code of Aethelberht of Kent, for example, if a man violated another man's wife he had to buy a new wife for the injured husband. Although Christine Fell indicated that by the ninth century the compensation paid for sexual offences to a free woman did get paid to the woman herself (Fell, 1984: 63), the overall tenor of the laws suggested that Klinck was right: that women in the early Anglo-Saxon period were subject to male authority and regarded not as individual entities in law but as part of the identity of both their kindred and their husband (Hollis, 1992).

The introduction of Christianity brought with it many changes, including the greater use of written documents, so that much of the evidence relating to women comes from the tenth and eleventh centuries. Whereas in the time of Aethelberht (king of Kent *c*. 535–616) women had little alternative to marriage, by the time of Cnut (king 1016–35) the religious life was attracting a significant number of women. Although wives were still repudiated, now they might be sent to one of the new monasteries as well as returned to their kin. The other major, and perhaps more important, change in society was the growth in royal power as the previously separated Anglo-Saxon kingdoms were forged into a single unit. Did this mean, as Klinck believes, that women were less subject to male authority and no longer under the guardianship of their kin? In support of her argument Klinck cites the laws of Cnut that a widow was under the protection of God and the king and that after a mandatory twelve-month period of remaining single she was permitted to make her own choice of life: to remarry, to enter a nunnery, or continue single (Klinck, 1982). Pauline Stafford has suggested that these particular laws of Cnut form a kind of coronation charter in reaction to the activities of earlier kings. His insistence that widows should not be remarried against their will also implies that in previous years kings Aethelred and perhaps Edgar had exploited their rights of lordship to the full and to gain allies had married widows and heiresses without their consent (Stafford, 1982: 189). The intervention of the king could work against women as well as for them.

Historians who believe in the equality and high status enjoyed by Anglo-Saxon women point to their control over property. Following the path established by Doris Mary Stenton, Christine Fell states that a woman had personal control over the morning gift that she had received from the bridegroom and his family after her marriage, so that she could 'give away, sell or bequeath' it as she chose. Fell goes on to assert that women 'moved in the world of landed property with as much assurance and as full rights as the men of their family' (Fell, 1984: 57, 95). The evidence that is always cited for a woman's rights over her morning gift is an early tenth-century land transaction at Fonthill in which a woman asserts her freedom to sell her morning gift. But a close look at the context of the case shows that it was in the interests of the purchaser of the land to emphasize a freedom of disposal that may have been far more debatable (Stafford, 1994: 238). Marriage settlements made on brides were usually in their husband's hands during their lifetime. Thus in the case of a married woman, her husband managed her dowry and morning gift and could do with it whatever he wished except permanently alienate it from his wife's possession (Meyer, 1979). Furthermore, widows generally had only a life interest in any land that they had been given. During their lifetime they could enjoy its revenues, but they could not alienate it, and on their death it passed to their husband's heirs. Moreover, as kings acquired the legal right of forfeiture, all land – including morning gifts – might be lost to the crown. Cnut, for example, legislated that a morning gift, together with any other land that a woman received from her husband, would be forfeit if the woman remarried within a year. While such legislation can be interpreted as protecting women – providing a disincentive to a forced remarriage – it does show that a widow's control over her property was by no means absolute.

Similar disagreements occur concerning the significance of female inheritance. Using the evidence of wills and charters Fell came to the conclusion that 'wives and daughters inherited and held property independently and separately from husband and father' (Fell, 1984: 76). It is true that some men in their wills left land and other valuables to their female kin – their mothers, sisters, daughters and more remote kinswomen as well as wives. Widows likewise made gifts to daughters and other female relatives. But the women who inherited land often received only a life interest with reversions to male kin, or to the church, if they died childless. Moreover, in some cases widows, in their wills, were primarily implementing arrangements made earlier by their fathers and husbands. Aelfgar, in charge of the county of Essex by virtue of his office as ealdorman, for example, had two daughters and no sons. Worried, perhaps, that they might be married to men not of his choosing, but to men of his lord the king's choosing, he tied the bequests made to them to any children that they might have and, failing such offspring, to churches for prayers for his soul and those of his ancestors. The daughters, one of whom, Aelfflaed, married Byrhtnoth, the hero of the battle of Maldon, did not have totally free disposition of their lands. Their own wills as widows show them primarily carrying out their father's wishes, although they were able to alter the direction of individual bequests as well as freely to dispose of other lands they had acquired (Stafford, 1989: 175; 1993). Thus by the tenth century a few women clearly did have some control over property and could will it to whomsoever they wished. These women, however, all belonged to the social elite. There is no evidence that the majority of Anglo-Saxon women enjoyed such gifts.

Since these early laws were not codifications of existing customs, practices which were well understood by contemporaries remain undocumented. Thus not one of the collections of laws provides a specific reference to inheritance rules. These rules varied according to the part of the country and the tenure by which land was held, but by the tenth century inheritance was patrilineal. In general the eldest son took everything, but in Kent, where special customs called 'gavelkind' prevailed, sons shared the land equally. The freedom to alienate property to whomsoever one wished belonged primarily to land that was held by a charter of 'book right', a right that originated only with the crown but once possessed could be passed on to heirs and others. Thus by the time of Domesday the free disposition of land that had originally been conferred by royal charters was enjoyed by quite ordinary commoners as well as nobles (Reynolds, 1994: 332–41). Yet it was kings and nobles, not ordinary folk, who either granted, or in the case of nobles transferred, land held by book right to their female kin. These women clearly enjoyed greater power and independence than other women of their class. They could sell or exchange their property or bestow it outside the kin group, perhaps on a monastic community. Yet in the same way as male holders of land held by book right, the women were responsible for carrying out royal policy and could forfeit the land for crimes such as theft, or for practising witchcraft and magic (Meyer, 1979). Moreover, they received these privileges, not because they had an inherent right, but simply because of their membership and association with the family of the monarchy or one of the earls. Their situation tells us little about the status of other Anglo-Saxon women.

It is clear that grants of land could be made to women, but for most of the period there is no indication how commonly or how rarely this occurred. The situation described in Domesday has, however, been analysed by both Meyer and Stafford. Meyer shows that in 1066 no more than 5 per cent of the total area of land recorded was in the hands of women. Moreover, of that 5 per cent of land, about half was in the hands of three female members of the family of earl Godwin – his widow Gytha, his daughter Queen Edith and the concubine, Edith the Fair, of his son Earl Harald. It seems as if the Godwins were using their womenfolk, on whose support they could rely, to bolster and consolidate family prestige and power (Meyer, 1991). The amount of land these women held was far larger than would have been customary for women of their social class and was an isolated phenomenon. Under William the Conqueror, Gytha's lands were seized into royal hands, probably because she supported her grandsons in rebellion. Domesday, moreover, is not necessarily the most accurate guide to female landholding. Pauline Stafford believes that it underestimates the amount of land in women's hands (Stafford, 1989). A dowry in land, granted to a daughter on marriage, was always held by her husband and listed as his possessions. So too land granted to a widow, since it was held only for life, might be counted simply as a domestic arrangement. Unless the deceased husband had been a sheriff or other official of the crown, who could have the opportunity to alienate royal land, the widow's portion did not usually come under royal scrutiny and hence enrolment in 1086 (Stafford, 1989).

The Conquest did not bring about any immediate change in women's rights and status. Before and after 1066 noblewomen could claim land as heiresses and hold it as widows. Furthermore, before and after 1066 kings were intervening in noble marriage. Families likewise sought to manipulate the inheritances and marriages of noble women, sometimes with and sometimes without royal consent. Some women benefited from royal intervention and protection, but others lost. Before the existence of a legal profession the rights of females to inherit and the rules and practices governing the share of her husband's lands that the widow received were extremely fluid and flexible. But the constant tension between the interests of noble families and those of the crown stimulated a desire for greater clarity and definition. The legal reforms of Henry II facilitated standardization and by the end of the twelfth century the practices, although by no means rigid, were more clear-cut.

According to Glanvill, a lawyer of the 1180s, the widow's portion of freehold land (her dower) could be given only in a valid marriage and it was to be given at the church door at the time of the wedding. The widow, however, had only a life interest in the estate and on her death it did not pass to her heirs but rather to the heirs of her husband. In some cases dower was made up of specifically nominated property, which could include money, rents, services or chattels in addition to land, but in other cases the widow simply had a claim to a share of the land of which her husband had legal possession (seisin) on the day of the marriage. In neither case did a wife have possession during her husband's lifetime, but if she had received nominated lands, upon her husband's death she could enter them at once if they were vacant. Otherwise she had to claim her share from the heir, but if he failed to provide it she could bring pleas before the county court, and ultimately the king's central court at Westminster. These pleas reveal that a number of second and third wives were forced to litigate with the sons of first wives, so that clearly in practice there was still room for flexibility and adjustment (Loengard, 1985). The size of the share (either a third or a half) depended on the tenure by which the land was held.

Likewise, the rules relating to female inheritance for common law tenants were worked out over the course of the twelfth century. If a tenant at his death had two sons and a daughter, the elder son received all the land, although he was under an obligation to honour any allocation that had been made by way of dower or marriage portion. The heir technically got the land, however, not by any operation of the law, but because the lord gave it to him. This power gave a lord, and especially the king, the ability in the case of female heirs to make a choice and pass over an heir with an unacceptable husband. By the end of the eleventh century the claim of women to inherit land in the absence of direct male heirs was clearly recognized. Thus daughters might inherit when there were no sons and sisters if there were no brothers etc. The woman, however, was seen primarily as a conduit, a means to transmit rights in land rather than with rights to enjoy the land for herself. It was always her husband who performed homage and was responsible for the services. Henry I in his coronation charter promised not to abuse his power over widows and heiresses and he enjoined his barons to treat their tenants in the same way. In the case of a single heiress he promised that he would marry her with her land and that he would do so with proper consultation – the counsel of his barons. In practice this meant that the whole inheritance was given with the daughter to the man chosen as her husband. Nothing in Henry's pronouncement indicates that several unmarried daughters would all be heirs and nothing is said about freedom of choice for the daughter. If there was more than one daughter surviving the lord chose one, but which one he chose could depend on her husband as much as her seniority. Furthermore, if the heiress was subsequently widowed a lord had the power to pass her over and give the lands directly to her sons. Subsequently, lords lost some of this discretionary power. Widowed heiresses gained the right to be left in possession. The eldest daughter and her husband were able to claim the whole inheritance, but with the understanding that any younger sisters would be granted a share in the estate. This vague understanding seems to have hardened somewhat in the 1130s and 1140s when a ruling occurred that 'where there is no son, the daughters divide their father's lands by spindles, and the elder cannot take from the younger her half of the land without violence and injury'. This ruling, however, is known from just a single charter reference and it is not clear what produced it or how widely it was followed. Nor does it affect the lord's power to choose husbands for the heiresses (Holt, 1985; Milsom, 1981; Waugh 1990). Furthermore, in the case where the eldest daughter had already married and received a marriage portion before her father's death the sharing of the inheritance was at first confined to the younger, unmarried daughters whose husbands had not yet been chosen. As Scott Waugh sums up, 'In 1150 women's inheritance was largely dependent on the lord and while there was a sentiment that an inheritance should be partitioned equitably, there was no mechanism for enforcing that principle. Lords and families through the assignment of marriage portions exercised wide discretion in the allocation of shares of the inheritance' (Waugh, 1990: 88).

Over the next century – 1150–1250 – the common law rules regarding dower and female inheritance were further refined. In the case of unnamed dower the right was expanded to include one-third or one-half of all lands that the husband 'possessed' at any time during the marriage. This change may have been signalled by the language in Magna Carta (1217 and later issues) that the widow would be assigned the third part of the land of her husband 'that was his in his life' (*que sua fuit in vita sua*). In the case of female inheritance the ethical principle of an equitable division that had been first enunciated in the 1130s became a specific rule. This meant that the heir could no longer be only the unmarried daughter(s) and that inheritance could no longer be only the property which the holder possessed at the time of his death. Land that had been given in marriage portions had to be considered. If co-heirs could not agree on an equitable partition of the inheritance they could request that a royal official value and divide the lands. Lords lost their discretionary power to favour one sister and her husband over another.

The guarantee of an equitable share did not, however, necessarily increase the power and independence of the heiress, nor did the expansion in the size of her dower necessarily help the widow. The marriage of a young, unmarried heiress was still within the control of her father's lord and widows whose husbands had held from the king could be forced to remarry someone not of their choosing. Although Henry I had promised in his coronation charter that widows would not be married against their wishes, this did not prevent him from collecting money from men to secure marriages with widows. Widows likewise paid fines to the king for their dower and for the right to marry or not to marry. Henry II and his sons followed similar policies to replenish their revenues. Some of the fines were quite exorbitant. Thus it is hard to agree with J. C. Holt (1965) that the king's willingness to accept these payments indicated recognition of a kind of independence on the part of the widow. As J. S. Loengard has remarked, 'whether it was a step forward in the emancipation of women would seem to depend at least in part on the size of the fine'. It was not until the granting of Magna Carta (clauses 7 and 8) that a widow was promised that she need not pay anything to secure her rights in land – her marriage portion, her inheritance, as well as her dower – and that she should not be compelled to remarry and thus need to pay a fine to remain celibate (Loengard, 1985; 1993).

Much less is known about marriage practices among the unfree – either slave or villein. In the Anglo-Saxon period it may have been unusual or even impossible for the poor to go to the expense of bride-price, morning gift and feast, so that without a formal marriage ceremony they simply entered into a 'domestic association' (Scammell, 1974: 532). Lords sought to control and profit from the sexual functioning of female villeins and levied fines either for fornication – legerwite – or on new husbands for the right to marry. From the late eleventh century peasant families came under pressure from local church courts – the rural chapters – to conform to a Christian model of lawful married life. As this change occurred lords gradually moved away from taxes on new husbands in favour of levies on fathers for their permission to marry their daughters (merchet) (Scammell, 1974; 1976). Eleanor Searle, however, while agreeing about the introduction of merchet in the eleventh century, denies the connection with ecclesiastical marriage policy. She believes the function of merchet was first to control land tenure and subsequently to tax the dowries of peasant girls (Searle, 1976). There are, however, other possible explanations. Merchet may well have originated in England, as in France, from an acute concern with marriage outside the lordship, although it changed its function to a simple marriage levy over the course of the thirteenth century (Brand and Hyams, 1983). At the heart of the matter was control over persons, not property, although the loss of goods when peasant girls married off the demesne with large dowries could play a part in setting the level of payments (Faith, 1983). Whatever its origins, by the early thirteenth century it was common for a girl of a peasant family which held any land at all to be given formally in marriage and the payment of merchet was accepted as conclusive proof of villein tenure (Hyams, 1980: 187–9).

In looking at the whole period from 500 to 1250, it seems that Pauline Stafford was right when she called for a new periodization with the late ninth to the mid-twelfth centuries sharing a common range of factors that mark these centuries as distinct from the period before as from the period following. By the late ninth century Christianity was well established and an ecclesiastical reform movement was under way which stressed legitimate Christian marriage. Double monasteries had given way to single-sex houses and female convents were no longer centres of learning. At the same time royal power had grown and with it the power and influence of the king's consort, the queen. Yet any influence that the queen wielded was dependent on the goodwill of her husband or son and could disappear as circumstances changed. So too land held by women as well as by men could be forfeited to the crown. Kings, like their nobles, sought to manipulate the inheritance and marriage of women to their own advantage and in support of their own political interest. Both Cnut and Henry I promised that widows would not be forced to remarry. Neither honoured that commitment all the time. Yet in the early eleventh-century kings and powerful earls were willing to grant full control over land to female members of their family to help consolidate their political position. A few West Saxon abbesses also controlled vast estates. Such land allowed women to influence the lives of dependent tenants. Most wives, however, remained under the authority of their husbands: the men controlled the property. It was only as widows that the majority of women gained any freedom of action. Either side of 1066 women could claim land as heiresses and hold it as widows. But the nature of these claims had not been clearly defined and both nobles and the crown enjoyed considerable discretionary power.

After the mid-twelfth century an expansion in the number and variety of female religious institutions opened up new opportunities for women to lead a religious life, but did not restore either the learning or the independence enjoyed by seventh-century royal abbesses. The spread of royal justice in the wake of Henry II's legal reforms clarified the rights of widows and heiresses but did not prevent them from being married off to men not of their choosing. As Pauline Stafford reminds us, the alternatives were not control or freedom but 'control by lord or by family' (Stafford, 1989: 87). It was not until the passage of Magna Carta that a widow of a freehold tenant gained the right to stay single and enjoy her dower and inheritance without paying for the privilege. Finally the growth of a royal bureaucracy and an end to the practice of serial monogamy reduced the opportunity for queens to exercise an independent political role, but left them with the influential role of intercessor. Within the countryside work had clearly become gendered, with some tasks like ploughing and carpentry lying within the province of men, and other tasks like laundry and the dairy seen as 'women's work'.

At no time in the early Middle Ages did women enjoy real equality with men. There was always a double standard with regard to sexual offences. In the legislation of Cnut, for example, a husband's infidelity was punished with a fine or religious penance, whereas female adultery was to be punished by a mutilation of the nose and ears, and forfeiture of any property to the husband. Men generally dominated the political and military arena. Although a handful of dowager queens did influence their sons, this power was exercised on sufferance and could easily be lost. Matilda, the daughter of Henry I, was the only woman who exercised authority in her own right and she never made good her claim to be queen of England. Nuns in the seventh century may have had access to a high level of learning and enjoyed the respect of their male colleagues, but they could never become priests. When the new educational institutions – the cathedral schools and ultimately the universities – came into being, women had no place in them (McNamara, 1994). Both before and after 1066 women held land, usually in the form of a morning gift or dower granted to widows, but occasionally by book right as a result of a charter. Yet the amount of land held by women was just a small fraction of that held by men. Moreover, the more land a women held, the more likely she was to be manipulated and controlled by male relatives or other lords such as the king (Stafford, 1994: 236). So long as women had basically only two life choices, to become a nun or to marry, equality was impossible.

3
The late Middle Ages (1250–1530)

The period of the late Middle Ages was distinguished from the earlier period by the growth and expansion of towns, markets, and general commercialization. Towns offered extended opportunities for female employment, both for wives helping their husbands to run a shop or business and for young girls working as servants or hucksters. Trades such as baking and brewing became first commercialized and then professionalized. Urban markets also provided a place where countrywomen could sell surplus produce and purchase manufactured goods. A further stimulus to female employment occurred when the population fell after 1348 with the Black Death and recurrent outbreaks of plague. At the same time the high death-rate facilitated female inheritance. Examples of wives and widows controlling large estates or continuing their husbands' businesses, taken together with the increased legal and economic opportunities affecting a wide spectrum of women, have led some historians to see this period, or parts of it, as some kind of 'golden age' for women (Barron, 1989; Goldberg, 1992a and b).

Economic activities of women

Women in agriculture and rural life

The high mortality after 1348 clearly provided increased opportunities for women to join the workforce, but very little is known about the actual conditions of work. Information relating to wage rates is remarkably sparse and little data exists about patterns of female employment over long periods of time. R. H. Hilton found countrywomen in Leicestershire in 1400 doing the same manual tasks as men – hay-making, weeding, mowing, carrying grain, driving plough oxen and breaking stones for road-mending (Hilton, 1975: 102). What is not known is how typical this often-quoted list of tasks was. Did women in Leicestershire carry out similar tasks in the 1380s, or the 1480s, and would women in other parts of England be following suit? Moreover, were these women primarily single women or married women and did this paid employment make these women, as Hilton thought, relatively independent?

Even before the Black Death women had formed part of the paid labour force. They had milked cows and ewes, spun wool, brewed ale for sale and worked as servants. At the time of the harvest a tenant, as earlier, was expected to bring all his family to the reaping at least once. Women might also harvest for fellow-villagers. Village bye-laws sometimes stipulated that if a man or woman could earn for his labour a penny a day, he (or she) was not allowed to glean (Ault, 1972: 30). None the less, except for tasks such as spinning and milking, seen as woman's work, women never predominated. In her study of the workforce on the manor of Ebury in the decade from 1330 to 1339 Sandy Bardsley found that women were hired for fewer days than men, and were paid an average daily wage of 1.58d that was about 73 per cent of the average daily wage of the male labourer of 2.17d (Bardsley, 1997). Apart from the *daye* (in charge of the dairy) the *famuli* on demesne estates – the ploughmen, shepherds, carters and pigmen – were all male. On many estates, especially ecclesiastical ones, weeding, hay-making and harvesting were *generally* carried out by male workers, but in time of emergency women might be employed. At Cuxham (in Oxfordshire) in 1290, after the meadow had been mowed by cottars, four women were hired to make a hayrick 'for fear of rain' (Harvey, P. D. A., 1976: 185–6).

Thus after 1348 it was perfectly natural for women to be recruited into the labour force when the need arose, but in many places they functioned as a reserve pool of labour, to be called upon in time of scarcity, and ignored when supplies of male labour were adequate. At Cuxham before 1348 only men were hired to weed. In 1349 to 1350, however, nearly all the weeding was done by women. Yet as soon as the male labour supply had been replenished, the men took over again. From 1351 to 1357 no woman was hired for weeding. In 1358 both men and women were used and in 1359 all the weeding was done by women (Harvey, P. D. A., 1976: 370–594). Likewise on the Sussex estate of Chalvington in the 1420s men were hired to weed, thresh and collect hay, as well as bring in the harvest. After 1430 a few women were hired for brief periods to spread and collect hay, to drive the oxen pulling the plough and to harvest. In 1441 eight female harvesters worked for a total of fifty-three days. Seven of the eight were married women and one was a widow. A few years later, however, in 1443–4, one woman and four men were hired to weed and another four women were hired at the time of the harvest. Three of the four were not-married women. The wives who were not hired may have been glad to have a little more time for other work, but almost certainly missed the income their employment would have provided (Mate, 1998). Clearly women at Chalvington never knew from one year to the next whether the opportunity for paid agricultural work would be available or not. When it was, only a small proportion of the available women in the community was likely to be hired and then for only a few days. Some women, not hired on the lord's land, may have worked for fellow-villagers. But those court rolls that record male tenants suing their neighbours for unpaid wages do not often mention similar breaches of contract for female workers. This absence suggests that women did much less casual paid work for their neighbours than their male kin.

When women were hired, how did their wages compare with those paid to men? In many places the records simply note a lump sum paid for weeding or for the harvest, with no indication of wages paid to individual workers. Harvesters were sometimes paid by the sheaf, or at so much per acre, and there is no means of knowing whether the money or the sheaves were divided equally among males and females. Some women do appear to have been paid at male rates, especially in the immediate aftermath of the Black Death. The female weeders at Cuxham were paid at the same rate as the men – 1 1/2d or 2d. a day – plus their food. In 1380 at Minchinhampton (Gloucestershire) female reapers and binders were paid, like men, 4d. a day (Hilton, 1975: 102–3).

Simon Penn, in his study of presentments made before the Justices of Labourers, also found that many female harvesters were being paid at the same rate as men – 4d. a day (Penn, 1987: 1–14). Sandy Bardsley, however, has suggested that where women's and men's rates of pay appear to be equal, what is happening is that the women were being renumerated at the same rate as boys and old men, or men with disabilities, who were generally paid less than the standard wage accorded healthy males. Her detailed analysis of information in the presentments made before Justices enforcing the Statute of Labourers in the East Riding of Yorkshire in 1363–4 clearly shows that female workers as a whole did not receive equal pay. Although the highest paid female worker did earn about the same as the lowest paid male workers, the average daily wage of female workers was 71 per cent of the wages of male workers (Bardsley, 1997).

The differential between male and female rates of pay obviously varied from place to place and from one time period to another. Nor is it clear whether the differential resulted from the fact that the workers were female and physically weaker or whether they were hired to do slightly different work such as binding the sheaves and stacking the grain. At Glynde in Sussex in 1372 the ten harvesters were fed 'at the table of the lord' and each man was paid 3d. a day and each woman 2d. (two-thirds of the male wage). In the early fifteenth century on the coastal manor of Pebsham, male harvesters received 4d. a day and female workers 3d. a day (three-quarters of the male wage). At Chalvington in the Low Weald, throughout the 1430s, the male harvesters were hired at 4d. a day and female ones at 3d. (Mate, 1998). Similarly, in the 1480s at Porter's Hill in Essex, studied by L. R. Poos, the sowers were all female and they were paid at the low rate of 1d. a day. Female harvesters, as at Chalvington, received 3d. a day while their male colleagues received 4d. (Poos, 1991: 213–15).

Taken as a whole peasant women's gains in the post-plague era *vis-à-vis* wage labour were distinctly limited. They were more likely than in the years before 1348 to be hired to sow, weed, harvest, or help with the haying, but such jobs were not available everywhere, or every year. Moreover, women frequently earned less than their male companions, either because they were hired for fewer days, and/or because they were paid at a lower rate.

Poos, for example, found at Porter's Hill that the mean employment and earnings over a year was 7.8 days for men, earning 24d., and for women 6.5 days, earning 13.1d. (Poos, 1991: 219). Occupational sex segregation remained as much a part of life after 1348 as before (Middleton, 1979: 147–63). Highly skilled, and therefore better paid, jobs such as carpenter, shepherd or plough-holder remained the province of men. Positions of authority and supervision, such as control of the dairy, or the work of the harvest, also remained in male hands. Female occupations were still worse paid than those dominated by men. According to the Statute of Labourers of 1444 a carter or shepherd was not to receive more than 20s. a year, a common servant 15s. a year and a woman servant 10s. a year. The one rural job over which women maintained a monopoly, that of dairy-maid, was extremely poorly paid – a woman hired on a part-time basis, just to milk, was paid at a 1d. or 2d. a week in the mid-fifteenth century.

As part of the general occupational specialization women were primarily responsible for child-care and housework – drawing water from the well, lighting the fire and preparing meals. This sex-specific division of labour has led Barbara Hanawalt to the belief that space was very gendered in the Middle Ages. Looking at coroner's rolls, she discovered that women had 61 per cent of their accidents within their home or village, while men had only 36 per cent in this limited area. Men were much more likely than women to die in fields, forests, mills, construction sites and marl pits. She therefore concluded that women's chief sphere of action was the home and village and men's was the fields and forests (Hanawalt, 1986a, 1986b, 1995). This hypothesis of spatially distinct spheres of activity has been challenged by P. J. P. Goldberg. He points out that the circumstances surrounding accidental deaths reported in the coroner's rolls do not reflect, as Hanawalt thought, everyday reality, but merely activities that were inherently risky. Men more often suffered death by misadventure in the fields because some of the work that they did there, such as carting, was much more dangerous than most of the work performed by women in the fields (for example, weeding, milking, shearing, reaping and binding). A peasant woman's domestic tasks never comprised the whole of her working life. Nearly everywhere wives raised pigs and poultry to provide food for the household. Women milked cows and ewes and manufactured butter and cheese. Vegetables such as beans, peas, leeks, turnips and onions, and also herbs, could be grown in both gardens and distant crofts and it was usually women who were responsible for planting, weeding and hoeing. Whenever such activities produced a surplus of goods, wives might take them for sale in the local market or neighbouring towns. Finally, spinning, an exclusively female occupation, was done on a distaff for most of the Middle Ages so that it could be carried out anywhere and was not confined to the home (Goldberg, 1991; Middleton 1979).

In the period after 1348 this work outside the home became even more important. With the shortage of people land became more readily available. Gardens, crofts or even whole holdings could readily be leased or bought. Labourers and craftsmen, who in the past survived on a cottage or 1 or 2 acres, could build up a holding of 5 to 15 acres. They were not solely dependent on their wages. Obviously not all *famuli* or craftsmen had holdings of 5, 10, or even 15 acres, but many did. Not all labourers were landless; nor were all shepherds and dairymen live-in servants. On the Battle Abbey manor of Alciston in Sussex throughout the fifteenth century shepherds and dairymen were always married men with substantial holdings. With the aid of family members they successfully combined farming and their paid employment. Carpenters and tilers did likewise. John Thatcher, for example, throughout the 1440s worked regularly for Battle Abbey as a carpenter on the Alciston demesne. He also held from the abbey a garden, croft and 7 acres in the common fields. In the 1450s he leased an additional 5 acres of demesne land. Although less is known about people who manufactured clothing – shoemakers, tailors etc. – evidence from Sussex points to the fact that they likewise frequently combined farming with the practice of their craft. With hired labour in such short supply the wives of these men may well have spent a larger portion of their time on *unpaid* work on their own land than did women of the same class before the Black Death (Mate, 1998). How typical was the Sussex experience is not yet known, but even in Essex, where L. R. Poos believed the majority of labourers were landless, he found some workers, who, like those in Sussex, relied on the fruits of agricultural activities carried out partly, if not wholly by their wives and children (Poos, 1991).

Furthermore, in the post-plague era many wealthy peasants – the yeomen and husbandmen – were able to build up large holdings of over a hundred acres. Their farms usually included a well-built hall and a number of outbuildings. On the death of the Sussex yeomen Thomas Bridge, in 1445, his daughter inherited a tenement that included a hall with a chamber annexed, another building (use unspecified), a kitchen, a grange, an ox-barn, as well as a stable for three horses. Such houses were amply furnished with feather beds, linen sheets, and a variety of brass, pewter and perhaps silver utensils and vessels. The men frequently worked for local lords as rent-collectors, parkers and the like, or joined with their master on poaching expeditions, or in forcible recovery of cattle and land. Consequently they were likely to spend more time away from home than men in their position had done in earlier periods. Their wives, left behind, would have been freer to make their own decisions concerning the management of the family land and its income. But they had to feed an expanded household, with at least some live-in servants, and whenever a family could not hire all the labour it really needed, it was the wives and daughters of the household who were likely to pick up the slack (Mate, 1998). Thus the greater availability of land was a mixed blessing for women. The extra land led to an improvement in many families' standard of living. They could eat more meat, and afford larger and sturdier houses. But the land, at the same time, provided more work for women.

Did a woman's contribution to the economy bring her power and independence as Hilton thought? Single women (i.e. adult women who have never been married) could be hired on a yearly contract as a dairy-maid or a servant. They might also find part-time work milking or harvesting, but they could not earn enough by such tasks to support themselves for the rest of the year and had to supplement agricultural earnings with work such as spinning, dressmaking or brewing. Some women may have earned enough by these means to pay their own marriage fines or even to purchase a small plot of land (Bennett, 1981; 1987), but the numbers appear to have been small and would have become even smaller as brewing became more commercialized and the not-married brewster disappeared (Bennett, 1996). The steady migration of young women from the countryside to the towns (both before and after the Black Death) suggest that opportunities for rural employment were limited. Those young women who remained tended to work as servants. They received their board and lodging, and a money-wage, but the amounts varied widely – from 2s. to 13s. 4d. a year. While they were working, they were very much at the beck and call of their employer, but if they did not need to give a portion of their wages to their natal family, they might have been able to save enough to provide for their own marriage portion, and to pay their own marriage fine. This independence would surely have given them greater control over the choice of their spouse.

Once married, did women's continued contribution to the economic well-being of the family bring them power within it? Hanawalt believed that peasant marriage was a partnership, with husband and wife each contributing their separate skills and their separate domains of labour. The majority of peasant men made their wives executors of their wills and they would not have done so if they did not have some respect for their wives' economic judgements during life (Hanawalt, 1986b: 16–17). So too Goldberg suggests that the cash returns from the sale of home-produced goods – spun yarn, butter, eggs, and the like – may have afforded women some independence of action and a 'very real degree of economic clout with the familial economy' (Goldberg, 1991: 82). He may be right that some women did control the family's purse-strings, but there is no guarantee that the majority of women peacefully enjoyed such clout. Furthermore, legally the situation was quite the reverse. A husband, as head of the household, controlled all the material resources of the family, including any goods that a wife may have brought to the marriage and any money that she earned through her labour or from the sale of goods that she produced (Bennett, 1987). If a husband wasted in drink or gambling what a wife had earned, she had no recourse in law.

Only in widowhood did a married woman gain control over her finances. Stressing the 'liberating' effect of widowhood, historians have assumed that if widows had perfect freedom of choice most would decide to stay single and independent (Hanawalt, 1986a; Franklin, 1986). Safe from the 'encumbrance' of pregnancy, they might often flourish in their new-found freedom. Widows, however, were not always completely free to choose. J. Z. Titow, writing about the thirteenth-century situation, distinguished between colonizing manors – where new land was still available for cultivation – and non-colonizing manors – where land was already taken. In the former situation, with the colonizing manors a widow's chance of remarriage was slight, since a younger son could always cultivate a patch of former wasteland or woodland, whereas in non-colonizing manors where such opportunities did not exist, the only way a non-inheriting son could acquire land was to marry a widow (Titow, 1962). Certainly on the manor of Thornbury, in the two decades before the Black Death, twelve out of fourteen second husbands were younger sons and none is known to have inherited or held land before marriage (Franklin, 1986: 200). The automatic connection between land-shortage and widow remarriage has, however, been questioned by L. Gates, who studied two non-colonizing manors of the abbey of Glastonbury for approximately the same time period as the Thornbury evidence. In one (Monkton) widows did remarry, in line with the Titow thesis, but in the other (Longbridge) they did not. The general unavailability of new land seems to have been less influential than overall socio-economic conditions. Longbridge, for example, contained a larger number of landless labourers and smallholders who could be hired by the widows. Gates concluded that elements such as available labour resources, social hierarchy, village industries, age at widowhood and dependants in the household, were all primary influences on a widow deciding whether or not to remain single (Gates, 1996).

The percentage of widows remarrying varied a great deal from manor to manor depending on legal as well as economic circumstances. Before the Black Death at Kibworth Harcourt, where widows forfeited their land if they remarried, only one widow remarried in the first half of the fourteenth century. They were presumably able to hire labour, or had enough unemployed male relatives to work the land (Howell, 1983: 34, 43). In contrast, in the same period, on the Cambridgeshire manor of Cottenham, where the lord was willing to collect large fines for the marriage of widows with land, they nearly all remarried (Ravensdale, 1984). Similarly at Halesowen, in the period between 1270 and 1349, 97 widows out of 154 (63 per cent) are known to have remarried (Razi, 1980: 63). At Thornbury, with a much smaller sample, the percentage of individual widows who remarried was 33 per cent (Franklin, 1986: 199). At Brigstock in Northampton-shire, as at Kibworth Harcourt, most widows remained single – only about 1 in every 13 marrying a second time – and at Iver in Buckinghamshire only 5 out of 34 widows (15 per cent) remarried (Bennett, 1987; 1992b). At both Brigstock and Iver an active land market and a diversified economy reduced the need for men to marry widows for their land. Most of the widows there seem to have managed their land quite successfully and do not seem to have had difficulty hiring the necessary labour. Some, however, leased part or all of their land and some, who were accused of illegally harbouring strangers, may have taken in lodgers for money.

Changed legal and economic conditions after 1348 inevitably affected the likelihood of widow remarriage. At Kibworth Harcourt the lord began to allow men to pay a fine to marry widows with land. The widespread labour shortage had reduced the pool of the unemployed and the abundance of land on the market allowed the heirs to establish themselves outside the patrimonial holding. In the short period from 1352 to 1363 five widows remarried (Howell, 1983: 34, 43). At Cottenham, on the other hand, as land became plentiful in the later fourteenth century, the number of widow remarriages fell off (Ravensdale, 1984: 209). Similarly at Halesowen only 26 per cent of the widows noted in the court rolls (10 out of 39) remarried in the period from 1349 to 1400 (Razi, 1980: 138).

In the fifteenth century land was still plentiful so that according to the Titow argument the rate of remarriage should have remained low. On the other hand labour was still in short supply, making it difficult for the widow to manage the land itself. On the royal manor of Havering, in the mid-fifteenth century, there were very few female tenants, which M. K. McIntosh attributes to the 'prompt marriage or remarriage of female heiresses and widows' (McIntosh, 1986: 173). On Sussex manors, in the period from 1422 to 1480, out of 153 widows, just over one-third remarried. Studies of early modern France and Renaissance Italy, however, have shown that after age forty the frequency of remarriage diminished (Bideau, 1980: 34; Klapisch-Zuber, 1985: 120).

When those widows who were young enough to have a reasonable chance of remarriage were separated out from the larger group of Sussex widows, the calculation produced thirty-two widows, of whom twenty-one remarried (Mate, 1998).

Why did men still propose marriage to widows at a time when other sources of land were available? The answer might be an unbalanced sex-ratio in the countryside. In places where a significant number of unmarried women had migrated to look for work, a young or even middle-aged widow would be preferable to no wife at all. A young widow could still bear children, provide meals, look after livestock and help out with agricultural tasks. She might even bring in additional income by working for wages or by brewing. In the fourteenth century ecclesiastical lordships like Battle Abbey insisted on collecting payments from un-free tenants who wished to leave the manor (see the section on legal changes) and this may well have discouraged female emigration. In the fifteenth century, when such payments were no longer being regularly collected, it is possible that a higher percentage of Sussex women were leaving the countryside, thus increasing the opportunities for widows who remained to remarry (Mate, 1998).

If it is easy to see why a man might propose, why did the widow accept and not choose to stay independent, safe from the 'encumbrance' of further pregnancies, and not subjected to the authority of any husband? With the general shortage of labour, it might not always be possible to hire sufficient males and, once hired, male labour might not respect women as proprietors and prove obstreperous when faced with her commands. Unable to punish them physically, a widow would be hard-pressed to maintain her authority. In addition a widow had constantly to guard her reputation against malicious slurs on her chastity (Hanawalt, 1993). Furthermore, the widow of a craftsman or labourer with limited resources was likely to face a drop in her standard of living on widowhood. Marriage clearly had its advantages, such as companionship, protection, status and frequently a larger income (Mate, 1998).

How did those widows manage who chose – or had no option – to live without a husband? Some leased a portion or all of their land. If the tenants were reliable, the widow was provided with a steady income and relieved of the burden and frustration of direct management. Unfortunately tenants did not always pay their rents on time and could reduce the value of the land by cutting down trees without permission. Some widows, therefore, managed their land themselves, but avoided many of the labour problems by concentrating on pastoral husbandry – breeding and taking care of pigs, cattle and horses. Agnes Gervays, at Brede, in the early fifteenth century, was constantly accused of trespassing with cows, bullocks, mares, foals and pigs. She sold some of these animals to fellow-villagers and when they failed to pay for them on time, she sued through her attorney in the local court. Similarly in the Sussex Weald, in 1453, four widows attended the yearly round-up of pigs, each with a fairly substantial herd – eight, six, seven and five pigs. Some of these widows also brewed occasionally, and a few widows became common brewsters (see following section). Finally a few widows voluntarily gave up their land in return for maintenance. If the widow did not have any surviving heirs, she could make an agreement with a fellow-villager. Agnes, the widow of the Alciston carpenter John Thatcher, leased her land for the first year of her widowhood. She then sold the tenement but with the provision that she could continue to enjoy the use of one acre of land, one chamber in the family dwelling, one half of the garden, together with the use of hall and kitchen and free entry and exit. Agnes lived with the new owners for four years until she died. Such an agreement, which provided the widow with the basic necessities of life, and perhaps some companionship, yet at the same time guaranteed her some privacy, with a space of her own to retire to when needed, was, for some women, more satisfactory than living alone (Mate, 1998).

Brewing and victualling

Both brewing and spinning were trades dominated by women and carried out in both countryside and town. Much more, however, is known about brewing than spinning, as from the late thirteenth century it was publicly regulated. People who wished to sell ale had to put out a sign – the alestake – and submit their brew to be tested. Local officials enforced standards of measurement, quality and pricing and made presentments of brewers for infringements of the assize of ale. These presentments soon became a *de facto* system of short-term licensing and covered the majority of those who brewed for profit. In some parts of England, however, most of the recorded names were males and elsewhere they were primarily female. J. M. Bennett, writing in 1986, believed that these differences in presentation reflected real differences in who was doing the brewing. More recently she has decided that her assumption was wrong and that the different sex ratios of presented brewers simply represent different clerical practices. Males were presented because they were heads of households, not because they were actually brewing. Although men, along with other members of the household, may have contributed to the brewing or sale of ale, it was their wives who bore the primary responsibility for much of the Middle Ages. Even in places where males were generally presented, some women were included and these were primarily not-married women, either single or widowed, although very occasionally a wife was presented when her husband was incapacitated, away or otherwise not acting as householder (Bennett, 1986: 20–36; 1987: 120–9; 1996: 158–71). Historians now generally accept that whether or not they were presented, women did most of the brewing (Kowaleski, 1995: 132).

In the late thirteenth and early fourteenth centuries brewing was a small-scale local industry that women undertook in their homes. As well as brewing for domestic consumption, many brewsters sold ale occasionally. In addition a few 'by-industrial' brewers sold ale to their neighbours on a more regular basis. At Brigstock, where about a third of the women who lived on the manor brewed for sale, 273 brewsters sold ale occasionally, and 38 brewsters worked more frequently. This latter group, however, accounted for almost two-thirds of the ale sold on the manor. Roughly comparable proportions of women brewing can be found elsewhere in the countryside, but in the towns the proportion of brewers was often lower. At Oxford and Norwich, for example, only about one household in every fifteen brewed for sale (Bennett, 1996). Profits, on the other hand, although generally low, were higher in towns than in villages. Because so many women brewed at some point in their lives, brewsters cannot be neatly categorized. Thus most brewsters were married, since most women were married, but brewing before the Black Death gave both single women and widows an opportunity to support themselves. Brewing was also widely dispersed across social strata. In some places brewsters came primarily from the better-off households and in other places, such as Redgrave in Suffolk, brewsters were primarily young, unmarried women with few resources, (Smith, 1984: 28) but, taken as a whole, the majority of brewsters came from families of middling status, who were long-time residents in their area. Although commercial brewing at this time was relatively of low status, was low skilled and poorly remunerated, Bennett believes that it contrasted favourably with women's other economic options (Bennett, 1996: 14–36).

In the late fourteenth and early fifteenth centuries the market in ale expanded. Wage labourers, whose wages had increased, had more money to spend. During the Hundred Years War wine supplies were disrupted and aristocratic and mercantile households switched to ale-drinking. To satisfy this demand brewing became more professionalized and concentrated in fewer hands. At Exeter, for example, in the late fourteenth century, although 71 per cent of households brewed at one time, only 29 per cent brewed commercially (i.e. more than ten times) (Kowaleski, 1995). Concurrently, especially in the towns, a sharper distinction arose between the producer (the ale-brewer) and the retailer (the tapster or tippler). Brewers were able to brew more ale because they could market it indirectly through the ale-seller. In addition to ale being taken away from the premises in the customers' own jugs, it came to be consumed on the spot in an ale-house, where customers could also buy food and talk with their fellows. Brewing professionalized more slowly in the north and west of England and more slowly in villages than towns. None the less, by 1500, in most parts of the country, the old system in which people took turns to brew their own grain had been replaced by a specialized, commercial system in which brewing for sale became a full-time occupation. Within the larger towns brewing was no longer carried out in the home, by household members, but in a separate brewhouse, by hired servants. As commercialization proceeded, single and widowed brewsters slowly disappeared from the trade. By the sixteenth century the only not-married women who brewed for profit were widows of professional male brewers, continuing their husbands' businesses. Other not-married women still worked in the brewing trade, but as tapsters who sold ale and as servants who worked in the brewhouses (Bennett, 1996: 37–59).

The not-married brewster lasted longer in the countryside than in the town. Although in the late fourteenth century the occasional brewsters quickly disappeared, some women took advantage of the new opportunities to become professional, full-time brewsters, although they still worked within their homes. Throughout the fifteenth century a few widows and single women can be found working as 'common' or public brewers in some villages and middling towns such as Battle. Most public, professional ale-brewers, however, were married women and were often quite clearly referred to in presentments as 'the wife of'. The latter had many advantages. Married women were generally better housed and therefore had more space in which to brew and serve customers. Through their husbands they had access to the capital needed to buy fuel and malted grain and to carry debts. They could also rely on the help of children and household servants (Bennett, 1996; Kowaleski, 1995). Eventually, however, both the married and the not-married brewsters in the countryside were replaced by male ale-brewers. In places where male heads of households were presented it is difficult to determine what role if any they played in the trade at a particular point in time and thus it is impossible to document precisely the timing of their takeover. Furthermore, brewsters were often married to butchers and/or bakers and towards the end of the fifteenth century husbands and wives managed some kind of general shop, selling meat, bread and ale. On four estates belonging to the bishop of Worcester male ale-brewers were presented for selling bread, candles and meat as well as ale (Dyer, 1979: 349). Did these men do the actual brewing or did their wives do it? In the Sussex village of Alfriston, in the first decade of the sixteenth century, wives were presented and it is clear that two women, Agnes and Marion Hayward, brewed ale and sold and perhaps baked bread, while their husbands worked as butchers. Twenty years later, when women were again included among presentments at Alfriston, six men were presented as bakers, and five of their wives were presented as hucksters of bread and beer. In addition there were two male brewers of beer and one male brewer of ale. If these presentments reflect the normal participation of women in the victualling trade there, then they were left with the subsidiary role of retailing goods produced by their husbands or others (Mate, 1998). What happened in other parts of the country awaits future research.

Within the towns, although not-married women did brew in the late fourteenth and early fifteenth centuries, they were a small fraction of the female workforce. Yet evidence such as the bequests of brewing equipment in the wills of females clearly indicates that a significant number of wives were brewing. At Colchester and Chester large-scale brewing was primarily carried on in the households of the more well-to-do (Britnell, 1986: 89; Laughton, 1995: 200). Maryanne Kowaleski, however, from the evidence of Exeter, comes to the conclusion that not just the wealth, but the actual occupation of the husband was an important factor in determining which families were likely to brew. In the late fourteenth century, for example, all the hostelers in Exeter brewed, and brewed on a more regular basis, than any other occupational group. So too almost all merchant and professional households brewed. They not only had the capital to acquire the equipment and raw materials, but their wives were not involved in their husbands' affairs and so had time to engage in brewing. Likewise the wives of braziers and goldsmiths and other metal-workers did not usually have the skills to assist their husbands in the trade and so would have more time for brewing than the wives of men in the clothing and leather trade such as weavers and glovers (Kowaleski, 1995: 129–36).

The whole brewing industry was to be revolutionized with the introduction and spread of hopped beer. Ale quickly deteriorated and the introduction of hops instead of spices produced a more stable and long-lived brew that travelled better. From the thirteenth century hops were being used by continental brewers and by the late fourteenth century hopped beer was being imported and sold in towns along the eastern and southern coasts of England. By the 1430s beer began to be brewed as well as sold in England. But since beer lasted longer than ale it was more economical to brew on a fairly large scale. This in turn necessitated the use of larger and more expensive equipment. The brew had to be boiled for longer than was necessary for ale and a better quality drink was produced with the use of a furnace – a special enclosed fire – instead of the liquor being heated over the open fire. The commercial beer-brewer thus had to purchase considerable amounts of fuel as well as the hops and grain. Finally, beer-brewing was very labour-intensive, so that beer-brewers generally employed more servants than did ale-brewers. Most beer-brewers were male (Bennett, 1996: 77–92). In places such as Colchester where, in the fifteenth century, the major brewers were 'beer-men', the urban, female brewster clearly lost ground (Britnell, 1986: 196).

Why were men able to dominate beer-brewing and gradually to take over ale-brewing as well? Bennett suggests that women's greatest disadvantage was their lack of capital. Married women had no legal autonomy so they were unable to borrow money in their own right. Not-married women, although they had the legal right to contract loans, could be seen as bad business risks, since if they remarried their new husbands might refuse to honour their wives' commitments. Yet the larger and more professional a brewing business became, the more capital was needed, for the physical plant, the equipment, raw materials and the ability to offer extended credit to customers. In households where men had other employment, both partners may have seen the women's work of brewing as less important than that of the male house-holder, and thus be unwilling to devote time or resources either to expansion or to switching to the new brew. Furthermore, the first beer-brewers in England were generally aliens and may well have employed alien, male servants so that women did not have ready access to the new technology. Even where women had the sole responsibility for the brewing, it was frequently their hus-bands, as male heads of households, who were presented as brewers before the courts. In places such as London, where in the early fifteenth century husbands and wives managed brew-houses jointly, it was the men who attended the guild breakfast, wore the guild livery, and took on the public responsibility of contracting loans, hiring and directing servants and negotiating sales. Once the trade has become a good trade for men, it was almost inevitable that they should take over full responsibility. Finally, Bennett suggests that brewsters may have suffered from the negative images of them as corrupt tradeswomen that appear in such artefacts of popular culture as the carvings on misericords (brackets on seats), as well as in elite texts such as Langland's *Piers Plowman* (Bennett, 1996).

While it is generally agreed that women dominated the retailing of ale throughout the later medieval period and into the sixteenth century, the number of tapsters, their origins and the profitability of their occupation remains poorly documented. At Exeter in the late fourteenth century the vast majority of brewsters sold their own ale and only a small group of women, some of whom may have been poor and unskilled, functioned solely as tapsters (Kowaleski, 1986; 1995). Similarly, at Chester in the fifteenth century the brewster wives of the well-to-do regularly sold their household's production in the cellars beneath their homes, but wives of middling status and some single women sold ale occasionally 'possibly from the doorstep' (Laughton, 1995: 203). On the other hand, at York just a few brewers sold their own ale with the aid of servants and much of the ale was retailed by tapsters, many of whom ran an ale-house. This group was predominantly female and drawn from lower down the social spectrum than those actually engaged in brewing (Goldberg, 1988; Goldberg, 1992a: 115). In the town of Battle the tapster as a separate occupation did not emerge until the middle of the fifteenth century and when tapsters' households were assessed for taxation in 1524, they were either assessed on goods worth from £1 to £2, or on wages and profits of £1 (Mate, 1998).

The practice of presenting the male heads of households makes it difficult to determine whether occupations in the victualling trades were gender-specific. Kowaleski and Graham believed that most baking was done by male householders (Kowaleski, 1995: 139; Graham, 1992: 126). It is possible, however, that in some instances wives were doing the baking as well as the brewing for which their husbands were presented. Female bakers were common in the City of London and some had their own bakehouse (Lacey, 1985). There is also evidence for professional female bakers working at the St Ives fair in Huntingdon, East Anglia, in the thirteenth century, and at Oxford and Nottingham in the fourteenth century, albeit in small numbers. On the other hand some of the women presented as bakers may have been working primarily as bread-sellers (Goldberg, 1992a: 109–11).

Female bakers may also have been baking horse-bread (made of beans and bran) or other low-cost breads.

Although males were generally presented as hostellers (innkeepers), many of them were involved in other work such as the buying and selling of textiles, which would have consumed their time and energy, so that their wives and servants almost certainly ran the innkeeping business (Swanson, 1989: 23). The number of widows in Exeter and Winchester who continued to run inns after their husbands had died also supports the argument that as wives they had been primarily responsible for the work of supervision (Kowaleski, 1995: 144; Keene, 1985). When the mayor and jurats (members of the governing council) from the Sussex town of Rye entertained visiting dignitaries in one of the inns, they reimbursed those responsible out of town funds. In the late fifteenth century these payments were made to the wives of the innkeepers. In the early sixteenth century, however, similar entertainment expenses were always paid to the male householder. This may mean that the women were ceasing to be in charge, or more likely that authorities did not recognize their contribution (Mate, 1998). Lacey also found that women of better reputation kept hostels and lodging houses in London (Lacey, 1985).

The position of the butcher, however, seems to have remained exclusively male, whereas the work of petty retailing was dominated by women. As has been noted, countrywomen brought their poultry, eggs, cheese and butter for sale in town market-places. Some townswomen bought these goods before they reached the market and resold them later at a higher price. Other townswomen sold poultry and eggs that they had raised in the gardens behind their house or shop. Many women sold fish, either as regular traders from stalls in a fish-market, or as hawkers in the street. At Nottingham, Colchester and York women are known to have traded in herring (Goldberg, 1992a: 107). At Exeter some women sold shellfish such as oysters and mussels that they had harvested themselves (Kowaleski, 1995: 139). When the city of Canterbury built a new fish-market in the 1480s, the Whitstable fishwives refused to pay toll. In London in the late fourteenth century all the eighteen stalls in the fish-market at Cheapside were leased to women (Barron, 1989: 47). Women also predominated in the sale of flowers and herbs. Most of these traders were married and worked just part-time, but some women seem to have worked as full-time hucksters, hawking whatever goods were available – second-hand clothes, pieces of cloth, lengths of yarn, tallow candles, fruit and vegetables as well as the staple products of dairy produce, bread and ale.

How significant were these changes in brewing and victualling? Female brewing before the Black Death was low-paid, low-status and carried out intermittently, and in the sixteenth century women's work was still concentrated in low-skilled, low-status work such as huckstering (Bennett, 1992a; 1996). The professionalization of ale-brewing, on the other hand, did help some widows to support themselves and offered a few wives an opportunity to carry out a trade that was separate from that of their husbands. The women who worked as public brewers, however, formed a very small percentage of the total female population, and in the process of professionalization a large number of women lost a chance to earn a little extra income. The gradual disappearance of the not-married brewster reduced the opportunities for rural earning and helped to push young, single women towards the towns. In the thirteenth and fourteenth centuries the knowledge that a wife could earn money through brewing as well as through spinning may have encouraged some rural couples to marry fairly young. When brewing as a source of supplemental income disappeared, couples in rural areas where other bye-employment was limited may have married at a later age than they would have done so earlier. Within the towns where the proportion of brewers had always been lower, and alternative sources of income greater, the rise to dominance of the male brewer may have had no appreciable impact on women's employment or age at marriage (Mate, 1998).

Urban women, the craftswoman and the trader

Women of all ages and all social groups were attracted to the towns. In some places in the late fourteenth century at the time the poll-taxes were assessed women outnumbered men. Gentry and noble widows frequently settled in a town, especially London. They lived on the rents of their country properties, but enjoyed the amenities of urban life – including the company of fellow widows and the services of a wide range of religious institutions. In addition many young girls flocked to a town in search of employment. Annie Abram, writing in the early twentieth century and discussing the situation in London, stressed the wide variety of occupations that women might follow, including barbers, apothecaries, armourers and water-bearers (Abram, 1916). She did not distinguish whether these women were widows, carrying on their husband's business, or young girls setting up their own craft. More recent historians, however, believe that the range of employment options for women remained slender. They found work either in service, in victualling, in textile work (primarily as spinsters) or in the production and sale of various items of clothing (Goldberg, 1992a; Carlin, 1996).

The term 'servant' referred primarily to young, unmarried individuals living under the same roof as their employer, but the term was very elastic and covered a wide range of duties. Domestic servants might spend their days fetching water, preparing meals, sewing or overseeing children. Within inns and taverns young women would be occupied dispensing ale and food. Some artisan households hired women to help them with their trade. Goldberg, in an analysis of poll-tax returns from five towns, came to the conclusion that female servants were most frequently found in victualling and mercantile trades and least frequently in the metal and leather trades (Goldberg, 1992a: 187). The poll-tax for Shrewsbury shows that skinners there had a large number of female servants, who probably helped to prepare the skins (Hutton, 1985: 93). At York dyers employed female servants to wash cloth preparatory to dyeing. Mercers and drapers also hired a large proportion of women, who may have served in a shop, worked with a needle or both (Goldberg, 1986: 25).

Women also worked as independent traders. At Shrewsbury there were single female cooks and some women earned their living as chandlers, in addition to the more common spinster, huckster and wool-comber (Hutton, 1985). At Exeter, a number of single and widowed women achieved some independence as tailors, hosiers (making stockings) and shepsters (seamstresses). Joan Shippestere, for example, both retailed and worked cloth for customers (Kowaleski, 1995: 153–4). Similarly in the unregulated suburb of Southwark, in 1381, 119 women practised a total of thirty-four occupations. In many cases, however, just one woman was mentioned in each category, that is one dyer, one fuller, one corviser (leather-worker), one glover etc. On the other hand, twenty-six women worked as spinsters, twenty hucksters peddled stuff from baskets, and there were twelve prostitutes, ten 'shepsters' or seamstresses and six laundresses (Carlin, 1996: 175).

The yearly earnings of any of these women is impossible to gauge. Hucksters may have earned more when prices were rising or in times of dearth than they did during the deflation of the mid-fifteenth century. Spinsters and wool-combers usually worked in their homes and were paid on a piecework basis. They were very dependent on the fortunes of the cloth trade and the reliability of their particular clothier. When the demand for cloth dropped, so did the demand for spinners, and some clothiers sought to ease their own financial problems by failing to pay or by delaying payments to spinners for work already done (Zell, 1994). Other spinsters might be exploited by unscrupulous employers, who used false weights when supplying wool to be worked on and paid in truck wages rather than cash (Goldberg, 1986: 29). In York many of the not-married women lived in the suburbs in 'mean cottages and cheap tenements' which does not suggest a very high standard of living (Goldberg, 1988: 107). Patricia Cullum gives several instances of charity being provided for poor women, working for their living, who were barely able to support themselves by this work. William Crosseby, dyer, for example, left 30s. 'to the poor women working at carding and spinning for me' (Cullum, 1992: 97). When the female householders in Southwark were assessed for taxation in 1381 they were rated as far poorer than single male householders, who in turn were rated as slightly poorer than married couples. The mean *per caput* tax paid by not-married women was 8.64d. compared to 12.29d. paid by single male householders and 13.23d. paid by married householders. Only a few female householders (6.5 per cent) could afford to keep servants (Carlin, 1996: 176–7).

If not-married women could not find regular full-time employment, they could end up in prostitution. In times of necessity, such as when the demand for spinning collapsed, a young woman could pick up customers in the street, or in a tavern, and take them back to her lodging. For such women prostitution provided a casual and occasional source of income, and Karras has insisted that they were not separated from the wider community (Karras, 1996). They dropped in and out of prostitution as the need arose. At Winchester and York, for example, the names of some prostitutes suggest that at other times of the year they worked as spinsters, wool-combers, cooks, dressmakers and laundresses (Keene, 1985: 390–2; Goldberg, 1992a: 152; Karras, 1996: 54).

For some women, however, prostitution became a full-time occupation and they either regularly took customers back to their lodgings or they lived and worked in a brothel. Most of these professional prostitutes were outsiders to the towns they lived in, and in London and its suburbs Flemish, Dutch and Low German women were particularly prominent. With no immediate family to provide help if they were seduced and then abandoned, or otherwise lost their jobs, prostitution might seem a viable alternative (Kettle, 1995). Some towns tried to control prostitution by regular fines and in others women were forced to practise their trade outside the town walls. In a few port towns and the London suburb of Southwark prostitution was officially regulated (Karras, 1989; 1996; Carlin, 1996). These women, unlike the casual prostitute, were clearly set apart from their fellows. They were often forced to wear distinctive clothing; they were forbidden to walk in certain parts of the town, and as 'common women' they were not allowed to have their own lovers. Although tolerated by society as a 'necessary evil' the prostitutes themselves were marginalized and exposed to the hostility and scorn of respectable householders.

Brothels, moreover, were seen as a source of disorder. In the late fifteenth century civic authorities in Nottingham and Leicester imposed new restrictions, and Coventry in 1492, as part of a campaign against harlots, passed legislation forbidding a 'sole woman' under the age of forty to set up house for herself. Goldberg suggests that such legislation was a reaction to the expansion of prostitution as women were increasingly denied access to other forms of employment in the wake of growing economic recession (Goldberg, 1992a: 155). This explanation, which fits the economic situation in the north of England, does not necessarily apply to other parts of the country where the recession had begun to ease, but action was still taken against prostitutes. In 1506 at Southwark eighteen brothels were temporarily closed and only twelve reopened. Both Carlin and Karras link this closure to the association in the minds of civic authorities between prostitution and criminal activities. As London became increasingly crowded, crime rates may have risen, or at least were perceived to have risen (Karras, 1996; Carlin, 1996). The common women, along with vagabonds, beggars and thieves, were even less acceptable as members of society than they had been earlier.

One reason for the concentration of single women in low-paid, low-skilled work is the fact that women rarely had an opportunity to be apprenticed to a trade and that they were often shut out from the trading privileges that went with citizenship. Although in a few towns unmarried girls were sometimes apprenticed, their numbers were extremely small compared with those of men and they tended to predominate in the textile trades (Bennett, 1992a). Moreover, this apprenticeship did not end with guild or civic enfranchisement as it did for males. Thus at Exeter, even though the town housed a very important leather industry, only a few women practised the work of leather-finishing with any regularity. As a result of her lack of civic economic privilege and access to capital and training opportunities the medieval Exeter woman was effectively barred from anything more than a 'minimal participation' in one of the town's most vital industries (Kowaleski, 1986: 152).

Within London, however, the opportunities for single women seem to have been greater. In the late fourteenth and fifteenth centuries girls in London could be taught to read English in small, informal schools and be apprenticed to a trade by the same method and under the same conditions as a young boy. However, girls here as elsewhere were most likely to be apprenticed to trades connected with victualling and textiles. They are known, for example, to have been bound to brewers, leather-sellers, and female pursers, throwsters, broiderers, and silk-weavers (Barron, 1996: 139–53; Lacey 1985). Occasionally too a young girl could learn a trade from her father or a wife from her husband. Thus within the City of London, where men engaged in a greater variety of occupations and above all in more specialized ones, Kay Lacey, like Abram before her, can point to women carrying out tasks normally the province of men, such as book-binder, book-seller, and even artist (Lacey, 1985). Such occupations, however, were by no means available to the vast majority of women seeking employment.

Married women, in all towns, frequently helped their husbands in the work of their businesses or shops and were responsible for selling the finished product. If a man was a weaver, his wife could operate one of his looms. The wives of shoemakers and glovers did much of the sewing involved in the manufacture of the goods. Even when men carried out a trade such as building construction or casting bronze or pewter that did not readily admit female involvement, wives could learn the business and be responsible for paying wages or hiring servants. The fact that craftsmen's wives were a crucial part of the skilled workforce shows up clearly in ordinances such as that of the York founders, who allowed one of their members who had no wife to take on an extra apprentice. Likewise restrictive legislation forbidding the employment of women usually exempted the wives and daughters of members (Swanson, 1989). By far the most common form of work, however, was serving in a shop, looking after the customers while the husband worked elsewhere.

Moreover, some married women carried out a trade that was separate from that of their husband. As has been seen, a wife whose husband was a butcher could work as a baker or brewster, and the wife of a mercer serve as innkeeper. In addition, many wives supplemented the family income by carding and spinning. In Coventry, knitting involved considerable numbers of women. In York the wives of butchers made tallow candles and black puddings. The small-metal trades of gold-smithing and pin and nail manufacture also employed women on a piece work basis, so that many of them could have been married (Goldberg, 1986). A few women were employed as midwives and sick-nurses and everywhere married women, as well as the not-married, worked as laundresses. In Westminster the wife of Robert Harrison, a smith, worked on her own account washing and mending clothes, including vestments for the parish church (Rosser, 1989: 198). Yet little is known about the conditions of the latter trade. Did the women, for example, wash the clothes or the linen in the residences of their employers or did they bring the dirty laundry back to their own homes (Jewell, 1996)? Wages, such as the 4d. a week that was paid to the wife of John Hayn for washing the linen of the household of Sir Henry Stafford, provided a useful supplemental income, but not enough to live on.

A married woman could claim the status of *femme sole*, that is, she could trade as if she were a single woman and she, not her husband, would be solely responsible for her debts. Although there was no legal bar to the kind of trade that such women pursued, they were effectively excluded from the more lucrative trades – butchers, mercers and drapers – by their lack of any formal apprenticeship. In London where women were encouraged to make a formal declaration of this status, those who did so worked predominantly as hucksters. Smaller numbers worked as embroiderers, cloth-weavers, brewsters, and upholders (dealers in second-hand clothes) (Barron, 1989). Occupational sex-segregation was as much in force for married women as it was for the not-married.

The London female workers about whom most is known are the silk-women. The craft involved three different processes: converting the raw silk into yarn, weaving the thrown silk into ribbons and laces and making up goods such as cauls for the hair, points for laces, and fringes and tassels. In many respects it was high-status work. To learn the art of silk-weaving young women had to serve a long apprenticeship – usually seven years. The work was extremely skilled. Some mistresses ran extensive workshops and received apprentices from as far away as Yorkshire. To purchase the raw materials and offer credit to customers silk-women needed plenty of capital. Yet they never established a formal guild. A girl on completion of her term of apprenticeship did not go through a 'rite of passage' to claim admittance to a powerful, well-defined community, but remained with her mistress until she married and was able to set up shop for herself (Dale, 1933; Kowaleski and Bennett, 1989). Silk-women, however, were clearly not averse to cooperation. The widowed Alice Claver relied a great deal on the support and friendship of two fellow silk-women. They took each other's children as apprentices, they witnessed each other's wills, acted as executors and made use of each other as sureties. When, in the late fourteenth century, their trade was threatened by foreign competition, the silk-women banded together and successfully petitioned both Parliament and the mayor. They never, however, developed a clear sense of work identity. Alice Claver, despite supplying the royal wardrobe with silk goods over many years, identified herself in her will as 'widow of Richard Claver, mercer of London', not as an independent silk-woman (Sutton, 1994). Their lack of guild organization has been explained by saying that the religious and social needs of the women would be satisfied by the guilds or companies to which their husbands belonged (Dale, 1933). But this merely serves to emphasize how households took their status from the male (Jewell, 1996: 90). As a result without any formal organization the silk-women were very vulnerable (Kowaleski and Bennett, 1989). When men began to move into silk-working, the silk-women could do little to prevent males from taking over a craft that in the fifteenth century had been a virtual female monopoly.

The activity of London women in trade led Caroline Barron to say that married women there were frequently 'working partners in marriages between economic equals' (Barron, 1989: 40). The question may be raised whether the wages or earnings produced by the wife were ever equal to those of her husband. The profits of the silk-women, although they were likely to be considerably greater than those of the humbler spinster, may not have equalled those of husbands who belonged to the aldermanic elite and worked as goldsmiths or mercers. A few independent brewsters may have produced an income that was in some way comparable to that of their husbands, but, as has been seen, many brewsters came from well-to-do families where the male earnings were likely to be quite large. The hucksters and spinsters, who made up such a large portion of the female workforce, worked long hours for low profits. Their income was unlikely to be equal to that of a shoemaker or master-mason who had undergone a long apprenticeship. Furthermore, as Barron recognized, the legal inequality between the partners remained untouched. Husbands, as heads of households, controlled their finances, including the wives' earnings. Finally few of the spinsters, hucksters or embroiderers could afford servants. The work that produced this second income had to be carried out in addition to their regular domestic tasks. Men who had other work were unlikely to take responsibility for laundry and child-care. Mate therefore concludes 'married women could well find that any economic independence was acquired at the expense of physical exhaustion' (Mate, 1998).

Urban widows often had the right to continue their husbands' businesses, including the supervision of apprentices, and some widows did take full advantage of this opportunity. At Exeter, Winchester, York and other Yorkshire towns a few widows were active in the cloth trade. In the accounts dealing with the merchandising of cloth (the aulnage accounts) a Wakefield widow, Emma Erle, for example, in 1345–6 accounted for forty-eight cloths (Kowaleski, 1986; Keene, 1985; Goldberg, 1992a). At Coventry, however, a widow was expected to continue the business only until the time that her son could take over. 'There was no question that widows might perpetuate the business by training up apprentices on their own account' (Phythian-Adams, 1979: 92). Moreover, not all widows followed in their husband's footsteps, even for a short time. At Shrewsbury the widows of butchers and bakers generally carried on the trade. Another widow made pots several years after the death of her husband, Peter the Potter, but the wives of dyers and tailors did not practise the craft as widows (Hutton, 1985: 93). Similarly, within the City of London at different times, two widows managed a bell-foundry, overseeing a large household and making bells with their own distinctive signs (Barron, 1994b). So too Matilda Penne continued her husband's business of preparing and selling furs (Veale, 1994). On the other hand, although some tanners in the early fourteenth century were prepared for their widows to take over the business, others preferred to leave it to a suitable male successor – a son, son-in-law or an apprentice. Even when tanners' widows were left tables, stalls or plots of land in the Tanners' Seld, the purpose behind these bequests seems to have been to conserve and transmit a scarce resource for the future benefit of minor children, not to secure the widow a means of continuing an independent activity in trade. Consequently in the early fourteenth century very few not-married women were active in London as tanners (Keene, 1994).

Urban widows, like rural widows, did remarry and for many of the same reasons. Hanawalt (1992), in her study of dower suits that came before the London court of Hustings, found that taking the thirteenth century as a whole about a third of the widows had remarried before bringing the suit, but in the immediate aftermath of the Black Death – the period from 1348 to 1379 – about one-half of the widows had remarried. Their new husbands usually came from the same or a related craft or business. The likelihood of remarriage, however, depended partly on the resources of the widow, and partly on her age. In the case of widows who appeared before the mayor and aldermen of London in their capacity as guardians of minor children in the period from 1349 to 1453 65 per cent remarried. Such women, however, were likely to be young and well endowed. Moreover, since the children were under age the widow and her new husband would have control of both her and her children's share of her late husband's goods and assets (Hanawalt, 1993). Older widows almost certainly did not remarry at the same rate. Margaret Stodeye, who was born into the wealthy aldermanic class, remarried within a few years after the deaths of her first three husbands, but after the death of her fourth husband, when she was well into her forties, she did not remarry and remained without a husband for the next thirty-four years (Rawcliffe, 1994).

Such high rates of remarriage may not have occurred in other towns, since before and after 1348 the ratio of males to females was frequently skewed against women. This imbalance, moreover, may have grown wider in those towns where after 1348 the prospect of urban employment increased the pace and the amount of rural–urban migration. At Coventry in the early sixteenth century, for every seventy-two males of servant age or above there were one hundred females. Remarriage was not common except for the very young wealthy widow and there were nearly nine times as many widows as widowers heading households there in 1523 (Phythian-Adams, 1979: 92). For the town of York, Goldberg, using information culled from a small number of wills, finds that apart from the period from 1418 to 1444, between 12 and 17 per cent of widows remarried in the fifteenth and early sixteenth centuries (Goldberg, 1992a: 267). Whether the percentage would, as he believes, stay roughly the same with a larger sample is impossible to say.

Not all towns offered the same opportunities for female employment. Young girls would have a better chance of formal training and a wider choice of occupations in London than in provincial cities. On the other hand, in port towns work such as fishing and servicing ships had little room for female involvement, so that women there had a narrower choice of occupation than elsewhere. Despite the shortage of labour, women were still found over-whelmingly in domestic service, and in the victualling and textile trades. Young, unmarried girls did not set up business as mercer, or draper, or practise a skilled trade such as shoemaker or carpenter. Only a few widows were able to carry on the trade or business of their husband, and even then they were frequently expected to relinquish control once their son came of age. The yearly earnings of women who worked as hucksters, brewsters or spinsters are not recorded, but were unlikely to have equalled or exceeded the income produced by a male journeyman who had served a long apprenticeship. Moreover, in order to make ends meet, urban women frequently carried out more than one trade – retailing ale, fish or poultry in the spring or summer and spinning in the winter. Even when wives worked fairly regularly as brew-sters, or as silk-women in London, they did not necessarily develop any sense of work identity. They were referred to in the official records and seem to have thought of themselves as wives or widows of their husbands and identified with their husbands' trades, not with their own. Furthermore, as seen earlier, the spread of beer-brewing, largely in the hands of men, eventually eliminated a major source of female earnings.

Demographic implications of women's work

P. J. P. Goldberg has argued that the increased demand for female labour in the post-Black Death economy allowed young women to support themselves through their earnings, so that if a suitable partner did not appear they were willing to delay or forgo marriage. Using descriptive data relating to deponents in York ecclesiastical cases, he came to the conclusion that most women did not marry before their mid- to late-twenties and that some women did not marry at all. A late age at marriage had important demographic consequences. Female fertility was inevitably curtailed. Yet, despite the labour scarcity, the economy was still expanding. When prices fell in relation to wages, the purchasing power of labourers and artisans grew. This in turn stimulated the demand for manufactured goods, such as textiles, that could be met primarily through the extensive employment of women. 'Women first filled those niches where female labour was traditional.' As the demographic recession continued in the face of endemic disease and declining birth-rates, the shortage of labour became severe enough to allow some women, in the second to fifth decades of the fifteenth century, to fill 'formerly male economic niches'. Eventually, however, the population shrank to a point where economic growth could not be sustained and agriculture and industry began to contract. Women were no longer needed in the labour force to the same extent as earlier. To protect male employment women were excluded from better-paying, high-status work, especially in the textile industry, and were forced into marginal and poorly paid occupations (Goldberg, 1992a: 336–7). As a result, at the end of the fifteenth century women unable to support themselves independently, chose to marry rather than stay single or married at a younger age.

Although this thesis is very influential, it can be challenged from a number of angles. Many of the women that Goldberg found marrying late, or not marrying, may have done so out of necessity, not choice. The evidence from the poll-tax returns clearly shows that in late-fourteenth-century York women outnumbered men. Not everyone could marry. Furthermore there are enough references to poor women working as spinsters, carders and petty traders to suggest that many of them lived in straitened circumstances. Servants were always in a dependent position and often worked for little more than board and lodging. A single woman, eking out a living, would have had to find the suitor very unattractive before she rejected him. As a married woman, continuing her trade, or adopting that of her husband, she would be likely to enjoy a higher standard of living, but also greater status and perhaps access to a wider social network. Furthermore, some poor urban women may have delayed marriage, not through any antipathy towards marriage, or to their prospective partners, but because without a dowry from their families it took them many years to scrape together sufficient resources to be able to set up house for themselves (Mate, 1998). Mate, however, does recognize that some women may have chosen to remain single; Goldberg likewise recognizes that some women might not have been able to get married. The difference between them is thus primarily one of emphasis. Were *most* women able freely to choose the lifestyle they wanted, or were the constraints of an unbalanced sex-ratio and a low standard of living severe enough to have limited the options for many unmarried women?

Charles Donahue Jr. has studied the marriage cases brought before the York courts, but has drawn somewhat different conclusions. Whereas Goldberg stressed the freedom of young women in urban society to engage in and to break off courtship, Donahue pointed out that most of the marriage litigation in the fourteenth century was initiated by women and that the majority of actions were to enforce a marriage. Women were also more persistent than men and pursued cases even when they had little chance of winning. He therefore hypothesized that 'Female litigants seem to have valued marriage qua marriage more than did male litigants' and suggested that 'Marriage . . . seems to have given women more in the way of security and status than it did men' (Donahue, 1993: 197). In the fifteenth century, although women still brought more actions than men before the ecclesiastical court, the disproportion was considerably less than it had been in the fourteenth century. Women also pursued their cases less persistently than they had done earlier and a larger number of them were interested in dissolving marriages rather than enforcing them. Thus he suggested that women in the middle decades of the fifteenth century may have been less dependent on marriage than they had been earlier. His reasons, however, are quite different from Goldberg's. In the mid-fifteenth century prices were generally lower and more stable than they had been in the 1360s and 1370s, so that a single woman did not need to spend so much of her capital to obtain basic necessities such as food. Furthermore, she could have inherited, or been given as a dowry, a greater amount of wealth, so that she would find it easier to live without a husband as well as have more to offer a partner. As a result more men and fewer women sought to enforce marriages in the fifteenth than in the fourteenth centuries (Donahue Jr., 1993: 204–5).

In addition, Mark Bailey (1996) has challenged the pivotal role assigned to life-cycle servanthood in determining rates of nuptiality. Smith, Poos and Goldberg all argue for an expansion in the number of servants in the period from 1360 to 1450 and above all for an increase in the number of unmarried women entering the urban labour force and staying there at least until age twenty-five. Since employers hiring live-in servants usually insisted that they remained celibate, young women did not marry until they left service (Smith, 1992; Goldberg, 1992a and 1992b; Poos, 1991). Bailey, however, has pointed out that there is no clear evidence concerning the number of male or female servants, either before the Black Death or after it, so that it is impossible to say whether the proportion of single female servants actually increased, or whether they stayed at work longer than they had done earlier. Contrary to the Smith–Goldberg thesis, Bailey believes that rural servanthood becomes *less*, not more, important after the Black Death as conditions for the wage labourer improved. Women, therefore, married relatively early, but supplemented the familial income with casual labour after marriage. Furthermore the experience of York was in no way typical for the country at large. In York the manufacture of woollen textiles was stimulated in the early fifteenth century by an expansion in foreign demand, but some other parts of the country were suffering from agrarian recession, deficient demand and an over-supply of goods. The period from 1360 to 1450 was not, as he sees it, one of unequivocal and consistent economic growth. If that is true, then the opportunities for women's work were more limited than Goldberg and Smith allow and their impact on fertility inevitably less (Bailey, 1996).

Behind the disagreements lies the problem of the paucity of the evidence. Little is known about conditions of employment, wages or status of various service occupations. Thus it is impossible to say whether female service in craft households carried higher wages than other kinds of work. Nor do we know anything about their status. But it is not intrinsically obvious that a female servant who washed cloth for a dyer merited higher status than a female servant who washed clothes or linen as part of her household duties. Even if Goldberg is correct that the second half of the fifteenth century saw female servants being excluded from craft households and other productive work in favour of more domestic positions, it does not necessarily follow that this change brought about either a loss of earnings or a loss of status. It may have done so, but there is no proof one way or the other. The distinguishing characteristic of a position in service and its great disadvantage were that so long as the position was one of living in, the servant was totally dependent on the goodwill of the master or mistress. That dependence was as true in a craft household as in other kinds and as true in the late fourteenth century as in the late fifteenth century. Some servants, living with kin, were well treated, others were exploited, but such circumstances bore no relation to the kind of work that was done. There is no means of telling which was the more common experience.

Despite these debates there is still considerable consensus among historians. It is generally agreed, for example, that women tended to marry at an earlier age in rural than in urban areas and that opportunities for female employment were greater in the towns than in the countryside. Women who left their natal home to seek employment elsewhere were generally freer to choose their own marriage partner than those who remained under the parental roof. Finally, no one would deny that some women in large towns such as York did not marry until they were twenty-five or older. The disagreement is over whether the *majority* of women, over the country at large, married late and whether they did so because they were earning enough that marriage was not an attractive alternative. Historians such as Bailey and Mate who argue that early marriage (in late teens or early twenties) may have been quite common in some rural areas in the late fourteenth and early fifteenth centuries, do not deny the existence of life-cycle servant-hood, but believe that a significant number of young women left service *before* their mid-twenties in order to marry. There seem to have been distinct regional differences. Within Sussex the custom of ultimogeniture, whereby the youngest surviving child inherited, and an age of majority of fifteen years allowed heirs of customary land to marry at an earlier age than they might have done where primogeniture prevailed. The ability to subdivide land held in the Weald also facilitated early marriage (Mate, 1998). How typical the Sussex experience was must await future research.

The labour shortage was by no means the only force affecting the position of women in late medieval society. Urban and rural women, as both producers and consumers, were deeply affected by the rise and fall in prices and the buoyancy and slackness of the market. Women were able to earn money as spinsters and harvest-workers only when there was a need for them. Thus in the late fourteenth century, when both the agricultural economy and the cloth trade was expanding, most women had no trouble finding work. In the mid-fifteenth century, however, much of the country was hit by a severe recession; the cloth trade collapsed, and the area under cultivation shrank. Where the recession hit, the need for female labour diminished, despite the continued demographic decline. With the high prices prevailing in the 1360s and 1370s, women who sold eggs, poultry and other goods in town markets might make considerable profits if they gained more from their sales than they were forced to spend on purchases. Conversely, during the deflation that accompanied the recession profits from the sale of goods (and thus their contribution to the familial income) diminished. Conditions that favoured one group of women, however, might hurt another. Urban women working as spinsters and sempstresses, and forced to purchase much of their food, were hurt during the times of inflation but benefited from the drop in prices in the mid-fifteenth century. The growing demand for ale encouraged the professionalization of the trade, and gave some women an opportunity to work as a public brewer while depriving others of a useful supplemental income. In seeking to gauge the economic gains, if any, that women made in the late Middle Ages, one must look closely as both the time period and the social group concerned.

Political power, education and religious experience

In the late Middle Ages, as in the earlier period, married women did not enjoy any public, legitimate authority. They were not elected to Parliament and were never appointed to offices such as sheriff, or justice of the peace, and they rarely served on local juries. Even within a village women were generally not appointed ale-taster or constable, and if the duty of acting as rent-collector fell on a tenement held by a widow, she was expected to appoint a deputy and not serve herself. On the other hand participation in political, military or administrative affairs frequently took men away from home for days, months or even years. Their wives were left in charge of their household and property and often enjoyed real power and control over affairs outside the home. Even when their husband was present, most women retained complete control over domestic matters and some women were able to influence their husband's actions. An aristocratic woman, or a queen, whose husband wielded extensive patronage, could thus significantly affect matters in a broad public sphere. A poor peasant householder or artisan had very little influence beyond his locality, so that his wife, however skilled she was in manipulating him, would not have much say in matters beyond her immediate village.

Judith Bennett, in discussing the position of peasant women in the early fourteenth century, makes a useful distinction between public power and public authority. In village communities access to public power was determined as much by the position of head of household as by gender, but public authority as 'recognized and legitimized power' was strictly reserved for males. Widows and adolescent girls who held land were required to attend the manorial court, and were liable for criminal actions undertaken by their dependants or themselves. They could also bring cases before the courts to recover debts and secure damages in the case of trespass on their property. Married women, on the other hand, had no access to public power, since their husbands acted for them, attending the court and pursuing and answering legal actions. No woman, however much land she held, joined a tithing or became a major office-holder. Furthermore, women rarely acted as pledges, or served their neighbours as attorneys or essoiners (people who brought excuses for non-attendance before the court). They were, therefore, barred from the opportunities that enabled men to solidify friendships and enlarge political influence. None the less, Bennett is careful to point out that although the dichotomy of private wives and public husbands was firmly established in medieval communities, this public–private distinction applied more to husbands and wives than to men and women (Bennett, 1987; 1988). This situation did not change radically in the late fourteenth century and fifteenth centuries, except that widows who were promised maintenance and/or an annuity instead of being granted land had no access to public power.

Rural women had multiple social contacts. Whenever they brewed and/or sold ale, visited the local market, or worked in the fields, they interacted with other people, both male and female. But did other social activity encompass both sexes? Barbara Hanawalt suggests that 'the tavern was the social centre for men and women' (Hanawalt, 1986a: 260). But although the misogynous literature depicted wives wasting their time drinking and gossiping at taverns, this does not necessarily prove that many wives actually did this. The value placed on female sexual purity was such that any woman who frequented taverns risked losing her reputation. Women clearly worked in taverns, dispensing ale. They had the right to attend, but from the late sixteenth century ale-houses were attended primarily by men. The same situation may have existed in the fifteenth century, since within the village there appears to have been quite distinct male and female activities. Men spent their leisure time playing at various ball games, dice and cards; in hurling stones, wood and iron, and in watching cock-fighting. Women may have watched these activities, but there is no evidence that they actively participated. On the other hand women may have created a separate space for themselves. When fetching water from the well, or doing laundry, women had the opportunity to exchange news and gossip. Moreover, at critical moments during a woman's life, such as during child-birth, a woman was assisted solely by her female kin, friends and neighbours (Mate, 1998).

Similarly within the towns public authority was confined to men. Women did not become members of the ruling council or its head, the mayor. Nor did they hold any of the lesser civic offices. Even though women could join some guilds and craft fellowships as members, paid annual dues and as widows continued to run their husbands' businesses, they were not eligible for guild office. Moreover, in some towns, such as Coventry, it was unusual for women to be present at either guild or craft banquets with their menfolk (Phythian Adams, 1979). The civic ritual that formed such an important part of urban life constantly underlined the peripheral status of women. Thus the lay dignitaries who accompanied the host on Corpus Christi processions were usually male.

Women, children and servants might watch or follow the procession as it wended its way through the town, but they did not join as official participants (Phythian Adams, 1972; Rubin, 1991). Yet women were not shut out from public power. As property-holders, unmarried women had access to the borough courts. They were liable for their own debts and they could sue others for trespass and non-payment. Urban women also spent much of their time in the public space, in the streets and in the market-place. Thus, more even than in the countryside it became important for women to guard their reputation. An urban tavern was a good place for a casual prostitute to meet potential customers. Respectable women who drank there ran the risk of being castigated as whores and prostitutes (Karras, 1996: 71). Thus although some women did frequent them, urban as well as rural alehouses were likely to be the meeting place for men (Mate, 1998).

Religious fraternities provided for the social as well as the religious needs of their members and were an acceptable forum for women to gather in mixed company. Patronal feasts at which single men and women were introduced to each other became an ideal place to meet a future spouse. Yet although women paid the same annual rates as men, and were active members of many fraternities, they tended to fill traditional roles. Female members of the guild of the Assumption of the Virgin Mary at Westminster watched over the body of a departed member, sewed liveries, prepared dishes for the guild feast and made or donated vestments for use at guild services. Yet the governing body of the guild, which served as a surrogate town council, was all male. Likewise, within the city of London, with its large number of fraternities, there is no evidence of women holding office (Rosser, 1984; 1989; 1994; Barron, 1985). None the less, women of all ages were able to attend funerals and feasts that became such an important part of fraternity life. Such meetings helped to cement close female friendships. Non-married urban women frequently lived in close proximity to one another and widows in their wills expressed their regard for their female kin, neighbours and fellow-parishioners.

Among the aristocracy, unlike other social groups, married women had access to public power. In the fifteenth century when aristocratic men left home on business, they were accompanied by male members of their household, and sometimes their sons, but rarely their wives. In a husband's absence, a wife took charge of running the household and the management of estates. Provisioning an aristocratic household was a major task, since the household included not only servants and the children of the house, but frequent visitors as well as a number of young people from outside the nuclear family who had been sent there for training. Although much of the work of day-to-day supervision might be carried out by officials such as the steward, in many households the overall responsibility for seeing that adequate supplies of food, fuel and clothing were always available lay in the hands of the wife of the lord. In addition, in her husband's absence a wife appointed and dismissed servants, disbursed funds and made decisions about issues such as the renewal of leases or the sale of grain. If the estates were threatened by actual disseisin (wrongful dispossession) or by legal action, a wife would have to respond quickly without waiting for her husband's orders. When an official of the rape of Hastings, for example, impounded some cattle belonging to Sir William Oxenbridge, his wife, Parnell, with two male servants, broke open the pound and recovered possession (Mate, 1998). Likewise Margaret Paston routinely collected rents, delivered legal writs and sought the intervention and support of royal justices. When necessary she acquired weapons and spiritedly defended the Paston property, and it was not her fault that she was ultimately ejected from one of her manors by an overwhelming force (Bennett, 1932; Haskell, 1973; Maddern, 1988). Although women were not directly involved in military campaigns, the defence of manor house or castle was a fairly regular occurrence. In 1338 Agnes, countess of Dunbar, defended Dunbar castle for nineteen weeks. As Rowena Archer pointed out, no undertaking that might normally be deemed the responsibility of men lay outside the purview of their womenfolk. They followed the same policies as the men and they did so in the same ways. There are no discernable 'feminine tactics'. Similarly their letters are rarely 'gender-coloured' with references to pregnancy or children. These fifteenth-century letters clearly reveal the respect and trust that the men had in the competent management of their wives (Archer, 1992; Jewell, 1996). Yet when the men returned home, however willing they may have been to listen to their wives, legally the final authority lay with them.

A wife, however, might be able to influence her husband's decision-making. Fifteenth-century men were well aware of the power of female influence. Sir John Paston, for example, continually asked his brother's help in importuning the Duchess of Norfolk to intercede with her husband in support of the Pastons. Margaret Paston was also willing to seek the help of the duchess (Archer, 1992). The world of the great household and the court conflated concerns that historians might label as either personal or political and 'virtually ignored the distinction between the public and the private' (Harris, 1990a: 260). Women as well as men were active in expanding and consolidating networks of friends and allies by the judicious exchange of gifts, favours and letters, and they were just as ready as upper-class men to take advantage of their kin networks to secure offices, annuities and other favours for their relatives and dependants. Honor, Lady Lisle, for example, through calling on her female contacts was able to place one of her daughters very advantageously at the royal court. While her husband was serving as deputy of Calais, she herself was constantly asked to use her influence to find places for young men with the garrison there. But did this power extend beyond the domestic realm and matters relating to the family lands, the household and personal friends? In the case of Honor Lisle it did not and she had no influence over the actual running of Calais (Hanawalt, 1988: 205–9). None the less, political affairs were not exclusively associated with men. At least one woman campaigned for the election of her son as knight of the shire and another woman reported on the state of the northern borders and Anglo-Scottish relations. Above all there is the example of Lady Margaret Beaufort, who conspired tirelessly in support of the claims of her son, the future Henry VII (Harris, 1990a). After he became king, Henry was willing to delegate authority to his mother and from 1499 to 1505 Margaret presided over a regional court, exercising justice in the Midlands (Jones and Underwood, 1992: 89–90). This example did not, however, become any kind of precedent for the granting of similar powers to other women. In general, aristocratic women had no public authority and, as in the case of Anglo-Saxon queens, such power and influence as they did exercise stemmed from the regard that their husbands and sons felt for their judgement. Yet it was the menfolk, and not the women themselves, who took all the credit or the blame for the actions that may have been instigated by their female kin.

As widows, some aristocratic women enjoyed even greater access to public power than they had done as wives. They now enjoyed full legal autonomy. When pursuing cases before the royal lawcourts, they were no longer accompanied by their husbands, and appeared either 'in their own person' or through an attorney. In addition to suits for the satisfaction of dower, and the collection of debts due to their husbands, widows steadfastly protected their property rights, claiming damages from trespassers on their land and poachers in their parks. Furthermore, if their jointure or dower included the grant of a manor or manors, they could exercise all the powers of lordship that had formerly belonged to their spouses. Although the manorial courts were actually run by a steward with legal training, they were held in the name of the widow, and any matters that needed clarification were brought before her and her legal council. Yet whenever a widow gave up her manors in return for an annuity, she lost those powers of lordship. Her ability to influence events in the political arena in some cases disappeared with the death of her husband, but whenever a son was willing to listen or to be influenced by his mother, she remained as powerful as earlier. Alice Chaucer, the widowed Duchess of Suffolk, continued to dominate politics in East Anglia long after the death of her husband. An aristocratic widow was as free to travel and entertain in her own home as she had been as a wife and could easily keep in contact not only with her own children and grandchildren, but also with female friends and male officials. Elizabeth de Burgh, Lady of Clare, entertained royalty, higher and lesser nobility (both male and female) and leading churchmen. She was able to use these contacts in support of her family and friends (Ward, 1992, 1994; Mate, 1998).

The position of queen was frequently linked with that of the Virgin. Thus powerful queens such as Emma had been juxtaposed with images of Mary as Queen of Heaven (Stafford, 1997a: 13). In the thirteenth and fourteenth centuries the Virgin was frequently described as a fountain of compassion and an intermediary between the laity and Christ. The most acceptable role for a queen came to be that of intercessor. Yet the very act of petitioning implied the queen's subjection to the king and the implicit acknowledgement that she did not wield any authority of her own. John Carmi Parsons, however, has argued that the queen's adoption of an intercessor's humble posture, which conformed to social and ecclesiastical expectations, allowed her to manipulate successfully behind the scenes and legitimized her crossing of the boundaries between influence and authority (Parsons, 1995a: 161). Parsons has shown that Edward I did allow Eleanor of Castille a significant share of the wardships and marriages at his disposal. Some she used for her female cousins, whom she married to English husbands, and others she used to reward members of her household or other families long attached to the court. At the same time she was able to expand the amount of land given to her use, thus providing a source of revenue for the maintenance of her household and for patronage that would be independent of royal largesse. This activity of land accumulation was encouraged by the king, and Parsons has suggested that in so doing Edward deliberately 'channeled the energies of a vigorous and intelligent woman away from matters of state' (Parsons, 1995b: 154). That may be so, but she did control affairs in these estates and when her officials used questionable means to increase revenues, she had to face widespread hostility. In contrast, Phillipa of Hainault gained great popularity after her successful plea to Edward III for the release of the six burghers of Calais due to die because of their town's resistance to Edward's siege.

A queen who did not follow accepted standards for queenly behaviour – who was not subservient to her husband and who did not restrict her activities to intercession and acts of charity – was liable to earn the disapprobation of contemporaries. Yet when queens were married to weak, incompetent rulers, they were presented with an opportunity and a need for direct, political action that could not be avoided. Both Isabella of France (the wife of Edward II) and Margaret of Anjou (the wife of Henry VI) showed themselves capable of meeting the challenge. Yet neither sought power for themselves until the political situation had deteriorated to such a point that there may have seemed little alternative. Thus it was not until the end of Edward II's reign, when the power and unpopularity of his favourites, the Despensers, had swelled significantly that Isabella began the negotiations with the count of Hainault for an army that she and her lover (Roger Mortimer) would eventually lead to England to secure the country from the Despensers and the removal of Edward II from the throne. So too until 1453 Margaret of Anjou lived as a dutiful wife and focused her energies on the effective distribution of patronage and the protection of household servants. Her letters indicate that she fully understood the power of her position and was prepared to use it to obtain favours for those whom she chose to assist (Dinn, 1995). Yet at this stage it was still a limited power. The severe mental and physical collapse of Henry VI in 1453, however, opened the way for a struggle between Richard, Duke of York, on the one hand and the queen on the other over who should dominate the government. In 1453 Margaret staked a claim to the regency of the country during her husband's incapacity. The claim did not succeed and York became Protector. But in 1456 Henry's partial recovery allowed the queen to regain power. York was removed as Protector and from 1456 to 1460 Margaret was the real ruler of the country, although the essentially passive Henry VI remained as titular ruler. Yet this power, owing to its special circumstances, was essentially ephemeral and disappeared with the seizure of the throne by the Yorkists.

Royal widows were in a particularly vulnerable position. As Joel Rosenthal has pointed out, 'royal widows were but left-overs, relicts whose potential for embarrassment and trouble was infinitely greater than any positive wisdom or contribution they might be allowed to offer' (Rosenthal, 1991: 182). In the late fourteenth and fifteenth centuries several royal widows were subject to periods of imprisonment or house-arrest. After the deposition of Richard II, his second wife, Isabella, was kept under house-arrest for several years before she was allowed to return to France. Joan of Navarre, the widow of Henry IV, was accused of witchcraft and imprisoned for three years by her stepson, Henry V. He may have imprisoned her in order to deflect her dower income into his coffers (Jewell, 1996: 135). Two other royal widows were forced to retire and stay confined at Bermondsey Abbey when their behaviour proved unacceptable to the new rulers – Katherine of Valois (the widow of Henry V) after the discovery of her secret marriage to Owen Tudor and Elizabeth Wydeville (the widow of Edward IV) after she was suspected of conspiring with Lambert Simnel (a pretender to the throne) against Henry VII. Life was no better for Margaret of Anjou, who after the death of her husband and son in 1471 returned to France to spend 'pitiful and impoverished years' there before her death in 1482 (Rosenthal, 1991: 181).

In the exercise of political power class was as important as gender. Although all women, by virtue of their gender, were excluded from publicly legitimated authority, aristocratic women had greater opportunities to develop their administrative skills and to exercise power, both as married women in the absence of their husbands, and as widows. Any widow with land, as head of household, had access to the law courts, but an aristocratic widow with substantial dower and/or jointure estates was likely to spend more time on legal matters than a peasant widow with just a cottage and a few acres. Women could also exercise indirect power, influencing their husbands or sons to make appointments or carry out policies of which the women approved. The greater the power of the husband, the greater the potential power of his wife, but that potential was not always realized. A dominant, powerful ruler such as Edward I left his wife a limited sphere of activity. Only a weak, incompetent ruler made it possible for a woman significantly to influence public affairs and such power was, in each case, short-lived.

To some extent the literary interests of women paralleled those of their menfolk. In the late eleventh and early twelfth centuries the few noblewomen who learned to read did so in Latin. Some are known to have become very proficient. Adela, the mother of King Stephen, read both Latin poetry and prose, and Maud, the first wife of Henry I, commissioned a Latin version of the voyage of St Brendan and a Latin life of her mother (St Margaret of Scotland). During the second half of the twelfth century literate women turned from Latin to French and command of the Latin language and grammar disappeared, even from the nunneries (Orme, 1984: 158–60). The court of Eleanor of Aquitaine, as she moved from Poitiers to England and back, played a dominant role in the promotion and diffusion of the ideals of troubador lyric poetry and became the catalysing factor in the integration of Celtic myths into continental literature (Lazar, 1976). By the end of the fourteenth century, however, French was ceasing to be the spoken and literary language of gentility and writers such as Chaucer and Langland had shown the power and flexibility of the native tongue. At the same time the springing up of schools had made possible a marked expansion in lay literacy.

Young girls, however, did not have the same educational opportunities as their brothers. Although in the fifteenth century many aristocratic women, taught by their mothers, could read English, they could not write it, and their lack of Latin excluded them from the formal education of the universities and the Inns of Court. Similarly, although some girls in towns such as London did have access to small, informal schools that taught them to read, they did not enter the new grammar schools that trained scholars to compose poetry and prose, both written and oral, in ecclesiastical Latin. How many women from the middle as well as the upper classes were able to read and write remains an open question, but Moran has estimated for the diocese of York a minimal lay literacy of 13–14 per cent (Moran, 1985: 181). It does seem clear, however, that in each social group fewer women than men acquired the skills of reading, and above all of writing. Sussex yeomen, for example, in their wills frequently provided money to send their sons to 'scole', but left to their daughters a cash marriage portion (Mate, 1998). When widows left money to endow an educational institution such as a grammar school or a university college, they furthered the education of males, not females (Davis, 1994; Jones and Underwood, 1992: 202–31). So it was with Queens' College Cambridge, the creation of Margaret of Anjou (wife of Henry VI) and Elizabeth Wydeville (or Woodville) the wife of Edward IV.

Women who themselves could not read might possess books that would be read to them. A few women owned lives of the saints in English and copies of the works of fourteenth-century mystics such as Walter Hilton and Richard Rolle. Other women owned Arthurian romances such as the tales of Tristan and Lancelot. By far the most common books owned by women were service books, such as psalters and Books of Hours in which familiarity with the language of the service would aid comprehension. Women also commissioned books, but female patronage was often hid under the name of the male head of household. The fifteenth-century poet, John Lydgate, for example, ostensibly produced works for the two husbands of Alice Chaucer, but in each case the real motivating force behind the commission may have been Alice Chaucer herself. On the other hand it is known that Margaret Talbot, Countess of Shrewsbury and daughter of Richard Beauchamp, Earl of Warwick, asked Lydgate to write a historical work, *Guy of Warwick*, celebrating the exploits of her ancestor (Meale, 1993).

Women were still attracted to the religious life in the late Middle Ages. Although nunneries no longer provided the same educational opportunities as in the seventh and eighth centuries, they gave women an opportunity to express their religious devotion and to develop administrative ability. Yet the number of female institutions had not kept pace with the expansion of population and there were roughly six times as many institutions for males as for females. Since women were forbidden to teach and preach, they had little place in the new mendicant orders, and just six female houses were established – five Franciscans and one Dominican – all strictly cloistered. In the early sixteenth century, at the time of the Dissolution of the Monasteries, there were around one hundred and fifty nunneries in England, but they were not evenly distributed. Houses of any kind were very sparse in the south-west and north-west, whereas in certain regions – Yorkshire, East Anglia, and the Midlands – where lesser gentry had opportunities to establish modest religious houses, nunneries were relatively dense. Roberta Gilchrist, however, in a comparison between male and female Benedictine houses, found that nunneries were substantially poorer than monasteries for men. When considered according to the number of inmates that each house was responsible for supporting, the majority of Benedictine nunneries (which housed any number between five and twenty inmates) held property valued at under £5 per inmate, whereas male houses had property worth from £10 to £25 per inmate (Gilchrist, 1994).

Our vision of female monasticism, however, has long been dominated by the work of Eileen Power, and above all by her vivid, delightful portrait in *Medieval People* of the prioress, Madame Eglantyne, with her fashionable clothes and little dogs

(Power, 1922; 1924). In this picture female monasteries became dumping grounds for undesirable daughters and burdensome, aged widows, who entered with little concern for their religious vocation. The majority of nuns came from wealthy, aristocratic families and needed substantial dowries to enter. These generalizations have been challenged in the study of religious women in East Anglia by Roberta Gilchrist and Marilyn Oliva, who found that in the diocese of Norwich the majority of nuns came from the families of the middling ranks of society – the parish gentry and the well-to-do urban-dwellers. The nuns were as likely to arrive with dowries of goods as with money, and some nuns were accepted without any dowry at all. Moreover, Gilchrist and Oliva are convinced that the women became nuns because they had a genuine vocation, not because of family pressure. Unlike Madame Eglantyne who had no head for figures and was a bad manager, these East Anglian nuns prudently managed limited resources and kept their houses from the chronic debt which plagued many of their male counterparts (Gilchrist and Oliva, 1993). Furthermore, formal, cloistered monasticism was by no means the only opportunity for spiritual life open to women in East Anglia. Some women worked as hospital sisters, and others joined small, informal groups and lived together under a self-imposed vow of chastity and poverty. Within the city of Norwich lived at different times from twelve to fifteen anchoresses and two or three female communities resembling Continental beguinages. The primary evidence for the existence of these informal groups comes from wills which made bequests, such as those to sisters (or poor women) dedicated to chastity. Unlike some Continental groups these women did not incur any suspicion of heresy (Tanner, 1984). It is possible that they were unique to East Anglia, but future research on wills in other towns may turn up evidence from other parts of the country.

A few women were also attracted to the unorthodox religious group known as the Lollards. Traditionally it has been assumed that women joined that and other such deviant groups because they were offered more opportunities for religious activity and expression than they could find in the established church. Margaret Aston, for example, believed that the Lollards promoted the religious and educational equality of the sexes, produced famous women preachers and, in the writings of Walter Brut, raised the theoretical possibility of having women priests (Aston, 1980). Similarly, Claire Cross stressed the active role that women played alongside men, making their houses available for heretical meetings, organizing book distribution and speaking out against sacraments, images and pilgrimages. She thought that the family orientation of the Lollards empowered women, making possible joint evangelism by husband-and-wife teams such as William and Joan White and Thomas Man and his wife (Cross, 1978). These interpretations have been disputed at almost every point by Shannon McSheffrey. She insisted that the ideas of Walter Brut were not part of mainstream Lollard doctrine and that in practice men dominated the movement as *public* leaders. Conventicles, where the people gathered to read and discuss the Scriptures and Lollard books were often made up exclusively of men, since it was difficult for an unattended woman to leave home and travel long distances to meetings. Most Lollard women were illiterate and had to rely on others to read the material in the books to them, so that they were not in a position to play any leading role. Evidence for the evangelistic roles of women such as Joan White is very slender and their prestige may have been simply a reflection of the activities of their husbands (McSheffrey, 1995: 58). Only one woman, Alice Rowley of Coventry, clearly enjoyed a public teaching role in conventicles of mixed gender. Rowley's activities, however, cannot be taken as typical of the movement as a whole. In general the family was the locus of most women's activity in the Lollard movement, but since Lollards saw the subordination of wife to husband, woman to man, as part of God's divine creation, women were left with supporting roles. They did host conventicles and, in an informal way, through conversations with family members, friends, and neighbours, did teach Lollard views on matters such as the sacraments and images. Leadership, however, remained firmly in male hands (McSheffrey, 1995).

The female mystic Julian of Norwich was acutely aware that her writing could lay her open to the charge of Lollardy. At the age of thirty, when she seemed about to die, Julian had a series of visions concerning the nature of Christ's passion on the Cross, his blood flowing down from under the crown of thorns, the drying out of his facial skin and other 'gastelye syghts'. At that time she was very isolated both as a visionary and as a female writer. Nicholas Watson has, therefore, argued that a short version of her visions – *The Revelation of Love* – was not written, as is usually thought, very soon after the visions occurred, but was in fact the product of many years of thought and anxious hesitation. In the 1380s writing in the vernacular, and objecting to image worship, became activities associated in people's minds with heresy. Julian was forced to become very defensive about her work: 'Botte god forbade that the schulde saye or take it so that I am a techere ... for I am a woman, leued, febille, and freylle.' Watson suggests that the first version was not finished until about 1388 and that the second, longer version was not written until the early fifteenth century. By then the long-standing English institutional suspicions of visions had begun to soften and several works by and about Continental women visionaries like Bridget of Sweden and Catherine of Siena had been translated into English. No longer so alone, Julian was able to write with greater confidence (Watson, 1993). What helped to make her work acceptable was the fact that she was an anchoress, shut up and confined from the world. Both Julian and the other notable, English, female mystic, Margery Kempe, were writing when theology was dominated by a male clergy. Women, who were forbidden to teach, could not speak as themselves, but as visionaries – the instruments and medium of God's voice – they acquired a voice otherwise denied to them.

Margery Kempe, however, broke with tradition when she refused the space traditionally allotted to religious women – the anchoress's cell and the nunnery. She attempted to live a quasi-religious life while remaining in the world: she wore a hair shirt, fasted and tried – at first unsuccessfully – to persuade her husband to live chastely. After she had borne fourteen children, her husband finally agreed on the condition that she would pay his debts. For the next twenty years Margery constantly left her home in Lynn to go on pilgrimages to different shrines in England, and to the Holy Land, to Rome, and St James of Compostela. She was strengthened in her resolve to lead this highly unconventional life by visionary conversations with the saints and with Christ. Thus at one point Christ is reported as saying to her 'I take no hede what a man hath ben, but I take hede what he wyl be.' Such a statement gave her license to 'refashion' herself (Beckwith, 1992). At another time, when Margery was worried because she had become pregnant again, Christ said to her, 'I lofe wyfes also' (Lochrie, 1986: 48). Furthermore, her social position, as a member of one of the most prominent families in one of England's major commercial centres, may have given her a sense of self-worth. As Nancy Partner puts it, 'Margery's brave stubborn defiance of convention and her ability to defend herself when she was accused of heresy took courage, a courage which drew of the reserves of pride and confidence belonging to a daughter of the Mayor of Lynn' (Partner, 1991: 32). None the less, the white clothing that she wore as a token of her dedication to God, her habit of instructing anyone who would listen and her loud sobbing at every verbal and symbolic reminder of the Passion angered many of her contemporaries. At the end of her life, she wanted to set the record straight. Unable to write herself, she dictated an account of her religious life to a scribe. Her dictation was ultimately transcribed, with some additional intervention, by another scribe, and produced what is usually described as the first autobiography in English.

The Book of Margery Kempe has been discussed from many angles by both historians and literary critics. Sheila Delaney, an avowed Marxist, sees the book as a 'document of the special oppression of women in early capitalist society' (Delaney, 1975: 109). Margery had no control over her body and thus, when her husband first refused to accept the vow of celibacy, had to endure 'legal rape'. The final bargain, in which Kempe gives up his rights, was a distressing mark of Margery's perception of herself as property. 'In this way, Margery, like any serf, buys manumission from her lord: the human property whose service she removes has its price' (Delaney, 1975: 112). Yet the same transaction appeared to David Aers as an example of the liberating potential of the market in that society. The practice of market relations, to him, increased the scope of choices and fostered the potential for 'increasingly differentiated identities and liberties' (Aers, 1988: 96).

In a very balanced study, Clarissa Atkinson seeks to understand Margery Kempe not only in relation to the social milieu of Lynn, but also with reference to religious developments. Kempe was influenced and encouraged by the examples of Continental, female visionaries and her religious life was neither aberrant nor even very unusual, but firmly within the tradition of holy tears and other practices of affective piety (Atkinson, 1983). Although aware of this line of reasoning, Nancy Partner is convinced that the convulsions and screaming which Margery experienced on her pilgrimage to Jerusalem had a deeper, psychological cause. Margery was a woman of strong and vital sexuality, but one suffering from suppressed, incestuous desire for her father. The first hysterical attack of screaming occurred after the death of Margery's father and to Partner it is symptomatic of a defensive struggle of Margery's conscious ego against knowledge (of her desire for her father) that she does not wish to admit (Partner, 1991: 38–66).

Were Kempe's spiritual experiences representative of late medieval piety in general, or only of women's piety, or were they too idiosyncratic to be either? According to Henrietta Leyser what marks out Margery is not the affective piety that she adopted, but the intensity of her response (Leyser, 1995: 222–39). The mixed life of action and contemplation that she followed was advocated for the laity by Nicholas Love, Prior of Mount Grace from 1410 to 1417, in his *Mirror of the Life of Jesus Christ*, and exemplified, perhaps, in the lives of pious laywomen such as the widowed Cecily, Duchess of York, and Lady Margaret Beaufort. Their days were apportioned between the services of their chapels, private prayers, reading and meditation, and the carrying out of their public duties – dispensing patronage, running their estates, listening to petitions, and giving alms to the poor and needy (Armstrong, 1942; Jones and Underwood, 1992). Within the towns some wealthy widows like Margaret Purdens of Norwich, who bequeathed psalters and devotional works by Walter Hilton and St Bridget, may have adopted a similar lifestyle (Tanner, 1984: 112). In this way the boundaries between lay and monastic life became blurred. The work of Eamon Duffy has emphasized the vitality of late medieval English religious practices and their appeal to women who relied on such rituals at critical points in their life. Candles blessed by the clergy for devotional purposes on the feast of the Purification of the Blessed Virgin Mary – Candlemas – were used as a form of protective magic at childbirth. Female saints, whose virginity gave them a great source of power to be tapped, were invoked as protectresses of the marriage-bed and as 'auxiliary midwives' and even as 'fire-insurance underwriters' (Duffy, 1990: 190; 1992). Lollard attacks on devotion to the saints may have helped to turn many women away from the movement (McSheffrey, 1995: 138–49).

The spread of literacy amongst the laity and the greater availability of reading material was to have a profound influence on religious practices in the late Middle Ages. Women from the aristocracy and upper bourgeoisie were able to possess service books – psalters and books of hours – that made possible private prayer and meditation. Religious books that had been translated (or were written in English) were also read aloud. Cicely, Duchess of York, would repeat and discuss at supper what had been read during dinner. Lollard women learned from books read to them as well as from private conversations. Margery Kempe was inspired by books read to her by a supportive priest. She was a unique personality, but her life does illustrate that a woman of determination did have the power to lead a life in accordance with her own beliefs. It should not be forgotten, however, that this was not an easy goal to accomplish. Delaney was right to emphasize that as a married woman, she was subjected to the power and authority of her husband. She could not live chastely, or go on a pilgrimage, until John Kempe agreed. She was able to succeed partly because of the wealth she had inherited from her father and partly because of the validation that she found in her visions and in the lives of female visionaries.

The legal position of late medieval women

Widowhood

To what extent did the position of widows improve as a result of the legal changes taking place? Janet Loengard has concluded that Magna Carta's rulings relating to the land provided for the maintenance of a widow (her dower) were generally followed in the thirteenth century. A widow was entitled to a share (normally one-third) of all the lands that her husband had legally possessed at any time during the marriage, not just the lands that had been his on the wedding day. Furthermore, her share was to be free from any obligation to pay the debts of the late husband and the widow did not have to pay a fine before she could receive the land, or if she wanted to stay single (Loengard, 1993). None the less, in practice a widow's position was far from secure and, as Sue Sheridan Walker has shown, she did not routinely receive her land at the hands of the heir. If the heir was still a minor, or some of the land had been alienated during her husband's lifetime, widows might have no option but to bring a case before the Court of Common Pleas when they were refused part or all of their dower or when they were short-changed in the apportionment of their property. In some cases the defendants then came into court and rendered the widow what was due to her, but more frequently they raised objections, of which the most common was that her husband had had no legal right to the property. Even though judgment was often given in favour of the widow, the process of securing a dower could be an 'engrossing, time-consuming business' (Walker, 1993).

During the thirteenth century, however, it became possible for husbands and wives to hold lands jointly. New acquisitions might be granted to both parties, or a man, at the time of a second marriage, might arrange to settle some of his land on his new spouse. So too at the time of the marriage of the heir, the groom's family could cede a portion of its estates and the land would be re-granted to the newly married pair, usually with a reversion to the heirs of their bodies. A widow could keep this land and enjoy the rents, even if she remarried. Furthermore, since she was already technically in possession of this land she did not need to go to court to claim it and thus might avoid some of the problems that Sue Sheridan Walker has delineated. If her husband died before his father, and thus before he had come into his inheritance, and no other provision had been made to endow her with land, the young widow would still have the land that she held jointly with her husband (her jointure). Because of these advantages, gradually, over the course of the fourteenth century, it became less common to provide a daughter with a dowry in land: instead the bride's family promised a marriage portion of money and/or goods and the groom's family provided the jointure in land. There was no set amount of land to be granted jointly; it might be as much as one-third of the grantor's estates, but it could well be less. The balance between the size of the marriage portion and the size of the jointure was determined in detailed marriage negotiations between the families concerned.

In the years following the Black Death a completely new legal development took hold – the use – which gave landowners greater flexibility concerning the disposition of their lands after their death, including the provisions they made for their widows, and allowed them either to expand or to undercut the traditional rights of dower. Lands were granted to trustees known as 'feoffees to uses' who became for most legal purposes the owners of the land, although the previous owner continued to receive its income. Since dower rights applied only to land which the husband had legally possessed during his marriage, if all his land had been granted to feoffees *before* his marriage, then at his death he technically had not possessed at any time real property on which dower could be assessed. He usually, however, instructed his trustees, through his last will and testament, to grant his wife a portion of his estates after his death to her use for life. This might be more than the one-third to which she would be entitled under dower, or it might be much less – perhaps no more than maintenance and house room or a slim jointure. A husband could also use this opportunity to impose conditions on his wife such as that she should give up the land in favour of an annuity when their son and heir came of age or if she remarried. On the other hand, if her husband had inherited or purchased land *after* his marriage that had not been transmitted through enfeoffment to use, she could claim dower rights over that land. Since among the aristocracy it was common for heirs to marry young in order to preserve the patriarchal line (Rosenthal, 1991), a number of widows had a claim to both dower and jointure, especially in the late fourteenth and early fifteenth centuries. This situation changed in 1536 with the passage of the Statute of Uses, which sought to end the fiction that trustees (feoffees) were the true owners of the land. If, as the statute envisaged, all land would again be held in full legal ownership by the beneficiaries and not feoffees, then it would become liable to dower. The statute, therefore, provided that any agreement made before marriage for land to be held jointly by husband and wife could act for ever as a bar to dower, no matter how much land her husband later inherited: if a woman married without such an agreement, she could collect her dower: if a man granted his wife joint ownership in land after his marriage, she was free to choose it or elect her dower (Spring, 1993: 47).

In discussing these legal developments, some historians see the lot of aristocratic widows as steadily improving and believe that widowhood was the most powerful phase of an aristocratic woman's life-cycle. A widow had full legal autonomy: she was not burdened with the need to maintain the heir or pay her late husband's debts and she enjoyed the revenues of her dower and jointure estates. If she was an heiress, she would also gain full control over her own estates. Many were very wealthy. Rowena Archer summed up much of current thinking when she wrote 'clearly the best years of a woman's life in the late Middle Ages were those of her widowhood' (Archer, 1984: 19). Archer stressed the havoc and distress that long-lived dowagers wreaked on the integrity of an estate. In some cases they did not even produce an heir: they carried property to second, third, fourth and even fifth husbands, collecting dower and jointure from each, and, although it was forbidden by law, they might waste the lands while they had them. Thus an 'untimely old mother could prove to be a blight on her son's fortunes' (Archer, 1984: 26). This emphasis on the wealth and independence of the widow and the corresponding burden and drain on the patrimony has been picked up and elaborated by historians writing about the gentry and their estates in late medieval England (Carpenter, 1992: 107–17; Acheson, 1992: 153). Even in counties such as Nottinghamshire, where in the early fifteenth century jointure settlements were highly 'circumspect', in the late fifteenth century sons and heirs 'suffered' from 'excessive' settlements (Payling, 1991).

In contrast, historians who have focused on the widow rather than the heir are aware of some of the disabilities that widowhood entailed and that widows did not always enjoy secure possession of their lands. Rosenthal cautioned against romanticizing the widow and insisted on the diversity of existence that widowhood entailed. In the fifteenth century, as in the thirteenth, the acquiring and keeping of a widow's dower was not particularly easy and depended on the 'smooth mesh' of many gears of government at the central and at the local level (Rosenthal, 1991). Widows often had to go to court to obtain or defend their dower and/or jointure and they were sometimes pressured or required to give up their land in favour of an annuity which was not always paid on time. Margaret, the widow of Henry Hussey, for example, was granted joint tenure in the manor of Harting, but her son Henry came with a group of armed men while she was at Mass in the parish church and took from her chamber a chest containing all the deeds of the estate. Eventually she remarried and she and her son came to agreement in which she gave up her claim to Harting in return for an annuity of £38.13s.4d. Many gentry widows would see their lifestyle and their standard of living scaled down, since their family income was no longer enhanced with the fees and gifts that their husbands had received for work as steward or legal counsel (Mate, 1998). Clearly, 'many women had very attractive possibilities as widows, but the realization of the possibilities was hardly automatic' (Rosenthal, 1991: 204). The examples of wealthy noble widows carrying land with them through multiple marriages need to be balanced with the number of widows (especially among the gentry) who were harassed by their husbands' heirs and forced to live in reduced circumstances.

At the level of manorial courts new legal procedures arose virtually 'in tandem' with what was happening in the common law courts. In the early Middle Ages land had generally passed from father to son(s), with just an occasional female heir, and provision was made for the widow in accordance with the custom of that particular manor. On some manors the holding was divided and half went to their heir and half to the widow. On other manors the widow could claim the patrimonial land, but not new acquisitions, and in some places she could claim the whole holding for life without any conditions. In general, however, the widow of a customary tenant, unlike the aristocracy, could keep the land provided for her maintenance (her dower) only so long as she remained unmarried and chaste. If a man wanted to marry a widow and retain her land, he had to pay a substantial fine to the lord. During the period from 1280 to 1310, according to Richard Smith, a 'significant transformation' of manorial justice occurred (Smith 1983: 95–128; 1986: 172). First a new process of surrender and admittance facilitated the permanent transfer of customary land and encouraged the sale and acquisition of land during the lifetime of tenants (an *inter-vivos* transfer). No longer did the patrimonial land pass unchanging from patriarch to heir. Thus a widow might find that on her husband's death she had no rights to any land. But, concurrently with the expansion in *inter-vivos* transfers, there came the practice of granting customary land, like freehold land, jointly to both husband and wife. After receiving an inheritance tenants could surrender all or part of it to their lord and ask that it be given to them and their spouses, sometimes with a provision for remainder to a named child of the marriage or a more general provision to the heirs of the couple's bodies. New land acquisitions, whether they came from the lord of other tenants, could also be given to both husband and wife with similar reversions. In the late thirteenth and early fourteenth centuries taking up land jointly became increasingly common on those manors in southern and eastern England that have been studied. What happened in northern and western England is at present not known. Joint tenure, moreover, had distinct advantages for the future widow. She did not forfeit the land if she remarried and if during the lifetime of the couple the husband decided to sell or grant the land to someone else, the manorial court (like the common law courts) formally examined the wife to make sure that she agreed with this transaction. In addition the necessary fees payable to the lord had already been met and the widow did not need to pay either the customary levy of the best beast (a heriot) or an entry fine in order to take over the land. Finally if the land had been granted without reversions, the widow was free to do with it what she willed, including sell it to non-kin (Smith, 1986; Mate 1998).

A further new form of conveyancing – the deathbed transfer – first appeared on some manors in the early fourteenth century and elsewhere not until the middle or end of the century. A customary tenant, lying on a sickbed, would summon to his or her bedside a 'third party' (usually a manorial official) as well as other tenants of the manor who could serve as witnesses, and make an oral disposition of his landed assets in the case of death. The official 'third party' was responsible for attending the next court and ensuring that the wishes of the deceased were carried out through the procedures of surrender and admittance. This process enabled the customary tenant to make last-minute provisions for his widow and non-inheriting children and to fashion 'comprehensive estate plans for the devolution of property' (Bonfield and Poos, 1988: 420). Deathbed transfers had multiple applications. Some tenants used the opportunity to disinherit their heirs – sons, daughters, nephews, nieces or more distant kin – by requesting that their land be sold and the profits used for the benefit of their souls. Other tenants granted land to non-inheriting children, including daughters, or kin such as widowed daughters-in-law. A deathbed transfer could also be used to shore up an earlier jointure, or to add a reversionary clause, or simply to grant land to a widow unconditionally (Smith, 1991; Clark 1996). Consequently the extent to which women benefited depended very much on decisions made by individuals. The new legal procedures were open to all tenants, but not everyone chose to take advantage of them.

So far only a few historians have explored in any way the incidence of these new legal forms and their impact on the traditional modes of the transfer of land. Writing in 1976, before the appearance of either the Bonfield and Poos or the Smith articles, Barbara Harvey noted that the appearance of joint tenure on some of the manors of the abbot of Westminster marked an 'erosion of the rights of the heir in respect of the family holding' (Harvey, 1976: 299). But, since in the fifteenth century land was so plentiful, heirs could easily acquire other holdings, and in some cases never occupied the patrimonial land. Inheritance was no longer the major mechanism for the transfer of land. Likewise Richard Smith, studying a group of manors in the Home Counties and East Anglia, found in the early fifteenth century a major increase in the number of *inter-vivos* transfers to married couples. Furthermore, on these manors by the 1420s between one-third and one-quarter of the customary land that was transferred at death was done so through deathbed transfers rather than through the customary rules of inheritance. Widows benefited the most from these deathbed transfers. In some instances widows received larger shares than they would have done under the normal provisions of dower, but if the share was substantial – over an acre – it was usually granted with a reversion on the widow's death to a named heir. On the other hand if the widow received just a cottage and curtilage she frequently had full rights over it and thus could alienate it to non-kin. The combined effect of the increase in joint tenancies and deathbed transfers was to undermine the centrality of dower as the basis for the wife's security in widowhood (Smith, 1991).

Likewise on Sussex manors during the fifteenth and early sixteenth centuries dower clearly played a diminishing role in the lives of widows of customary tenants. After 1480, with the breakup and dissipation of the large bond holdings, it was rarely claimed. In its place came joint tenure, and to a much lower degree than on the manors studied by Smith, deathbed transfers. Even so, at the end of the fifteenth century only about 50 per cent of the *inter-vivos* transfers were going to married couples. Widows who did hold land, whether by joint tenure or a deathbed transfer, were in a stronger position than widows in the early fourteenth century, since they could take their land with them to a second or third marriage. But in the cases when property went directly to the heir, a widow who did not have rights to land elsewhere had to rely on maintenance within the family home or the payment of an annuity. She could well have enjoyed less independence and less security than her forebears (Mate, 1998).

The rights of urban widows were potentially more limited than those of women of other social groups. Urban property could be freely sold or bequeathed during a husband's lifetime, and widows had no rights over this alienated land. Furthermore, like other widows, urban women could not claim a dower on land granted to trustees before a marriage. Thus their traditional claim to a share in the house in which they had been living and a half or third share of their husband's lands and tenements might be difficult to realize. Urban widows, like aristocratic widows, frequently had to go to court to secure their dower and met with the same kind of objections. In a study of London widows, in just over half the cases which were brought to a conclusion the widow successfully recovered all or part of her dower, but the process was 'fairly lengthy' (Hanawalt, 1992: 28). What happened to the other half of the widows who received only part of their dower was not discussed. Urban women, however, could hold property jointly with their husbands and keep these tenements after his death. Yet in the town of Battle joint tenure became less common after the middle of the fifteenth century (Mate, 1998). A widow who did not hold any property jointly, and who did not receive her dower, may have been left with little more than the use of rooms in her former home.

In looking at urban women, however, it is important to remember that the lifestyle of the elite was very different from that of the non-elite families (Kowaleski, 1988). An elite widow, in addition to dower and/or jointure, had the right to continue her husband's business, including the supervision of apprentices, for at least a few years after his death. She was, also, entitled to a share of her late husband's goods and chattels and these goods were hers absolutely to dispose of as she pleased. In the case of mercantile widows, where the husband's wealth might take the form of bales of wool or cloth, or debts owing to them, the widow's share – her *legitim* – could be extremely valuable. In contrast, the widow of a journeyman or a mariner, or widows of small-scale artisans such as carpenters, inherited very little in the way of moveable property. The family frequently lived in rented accommodation, so that the widow had no claim to property. Without the income her husband had generated the widow still had to pay the rent for her lodging, plus the food and clothing for herself and any young children, from whatever she could earn. Some widows may have had to move to cheaper accommodation at the edge of town and, if their children had already left home, had to share a room with another woman or live alone. In Coventry, in the early sixteenth century, roughly half the widows lived alone, many in extreme poverty (Phythian-Adams, 1979: 92). Similarly, in Exeter the households headed by women at the time of the poll-tax were much poorer than male-headed ones (Kowaleski, 1988b: 86).

Inheritance and marriage

The rules governing inheritance that had been worked out over the course of the twelfth and thirteenth centuries remained in force throughout the rest of the Middle Ages. As the population fell in the wake of the Black Death and subsequent outbreaks of plague, the number of common law heiresses inevitably expanded (Payling, 1992). The acquisition of land, however, did not often bring heiresses either independence or power. If she was already married at the time she received her inheritance, she, like all married women, was a *femme couverte* under the legal authority of her husband. Her land and its legal responsibilities would be taken over and managed by him, although he had no right to alienate it without her consent. The proceeds of the land, whether in money or kind, were legally his to dispose of, not his wife's. Her husband, not the heiress herself, often performed homage and fealty for the land and was listed in any rental. He also controlled all the goods that she brought to the marriage and could freely dispose of them, leaving his wife nothing but her clothes and her jewellery. So long as her husband was alive, a wife had no right to make a will, since all the goods theoretically belonged to him. Although in practice most husbands did not dissipate their wives' inheritance in goods, a few did, and their wives had no legal recourse.

If the heiress was still a minor and unmarried, her guardianship and her marriage became a source of profit to the lord from whom the land was held. The church's new ruling on what constituted a valid marriage did, however, provide some protection against forced marriages. Pope Alexander III (1159–81) decreed that what made a marriage was the consent of the contracting parties alone. Theoretically, therefore, neither families nor legal guardians could force young girls into marriage against their will. In addition, any marriages they themselves made could not be invalidated on the grounds that they had not received the consent of parents, lord or guardian. Wards had the right to refuse the marriages proposed for them and could pay to have free choice of marriage. Sue Sheridan Walker believes that a 'great many' wards exercised this privilege (Walker, 1982: 124). Likewise widows, who held from the king and could not marry without his consent, married men of their choice, and if they were sued, fined for forgiveness. So long as they received the monetary value for the marriage, lords did not usually complain. Families, however, were more directly concerned with the choice of marriage partners for their children and were willing, as in the earlier period, to ensure obedience through pressure. Most of the cases brought before the ecclesiastical courts in the thirteenth century for annulment of a 'forced' marriage concern constraint not by feudal lords, but by families (Walker, 1982: 124–6). Coercion, however, could take many forms, not all of them overt enough to constitute legal proof. Young girls were not always willing to stand up for their rights and gainsay a powerful parent or guardian. Thus some aristocratic women were likely to be married in their teens to men about whom they knew very little before their marriage.

Likewise, in the absence of male heirs, women could inherit land held by customary tenure. On manors where inheritance went first to the eldest son (primogenture) female heirs, as with free-hold tenure, divided the land between them, but on the Sussex manors where the youngest son was the normal heir (ultimogeni-ture), the entire holding went to the youngest daughter or her heirs. In the post-plague era, with its high mortality, inheritance through the female line could significantly affect the land market. On the manor of Halesowen, studied by Zvi Razi, before 1349 the majority of holdings were transferred to local villagers who were usually closely related through the male line. After the Black Death a higher proportion of holdings were transferred to im-migrants 'who were more distantly related to the deceased tenants and often through the female line' (Razi, 1981: 22).

Heiresses on customary land who were minors were usually given into the guardianship of their mothers until they came of age or were married. Although an heiress could marry a landless, non-inheriting son, in Halesowen heiresses were often married to heirs (Razi, 1996: 332). So too on Sussex manors, after the Black Death when land was plentiful, it was common for an heiress to marry a man who already possessed land and buildings of his own. She then settled on her husband's property and the maintenance of his property frequently took precedence over the maintenance of hers. But a tenant by customary tenure, holding at the will of the lord, risked forfeiting the land if he or she failed to carry out the necessary services or to keep the property in good repair. A married woman could thus lose her inheritance as a result of her husband's actions and she had little hope of redress (Mate, 1998).

Did the right of lords to levy a marriage fine (merchet) on their female, unfree tenants, give them control over such marriages, and the power to accept or reject prospective tenants? Eleanor Searle believes that it did, whereas Paul Brand, Paul Hyams and Rosa-mond Faith insist that by the thirteenth century lords simply demanded a payment for licence to marry and did not exercise any right of veto over the family's choice of a husband (Searle, 1979; Brand and Hyams, 1983; Faith, 1983). Although some lords in the thirteenth and early fourteenth centuries did direct unmarried tenants to marry and sought to find husbands for widows, on the Norfolk and Sussex manors that have been studied most tenants paid fines instead of marrying the spouses selected for them. Widows, for example could pay to remain unmarried or choose their own husbands (Clark, 1987; Mate, 1991: 96). Moreover, it does not appear that the lord's authority was meant to supersede that of a living father. Although heirs and heiresses were among those ordered to marry, they were generally orphaned or fatherless (Clark, 1987: 502). Marriage fines, moreover, might be levied on non-inheriting as well as inheriting daughters. In some places the fine was paid only by the families of property or more prosperous villeins, but elsewhere all unfree tenants were required to pay (Faith, 1983).

In the century after 1348 the old system of villeinage gradually broke down. Men and women of villein status left their manors to find work elsewhere and did not return. With labour and tenants in such short supply lords did not enquire too closely about the status of either their workers or prospective tenants, and people who claimed to be free were accepted as such. Other villeins won their freedom through residence in a town. Villein women married free men and their children automatically were regarded as free. None the less, the payment of merchet did not disappear overnight. On the St Albans manor of Park, although the number of payments declined after 1348, they did not disappear until the end of the fourteenth century (Faith, 1983: 146). On Norfolk manors in the 1380s lords no longer attempted to coerce peasants to marry, but tenants still paid marriage fines (Clark, 1987: 511). So too on Sussex manors merchet was regularly collected throughout the late fourteenth century, but became more sporadic in the early fifteenth century and finally disappeared in mid-century (Mate, 1998).

The general shortage of labour, however, opened up opportunities for female employment and some villein women were able to pay their own fines. Judith Bennett has studied the records of 426 merchet payments from 29 of the manors of Ramsey Abbey between 1398 and 1458 and found that the prospective bride and her father are recorded as paying merchets with equal frequency – each 33 per cent (Bennett, 1981: 197). Bennett is convinced that the women themselves were actually responsible for payment, since they were more likely to be asked to provide a personal pledge and their fines were generally lower. A young woman, however, was unlikely to have earned enough to pay her own fine until she reached her mid-twenties, so she probably married fairly late, but she may well have chosen her own spouse, since a large proportion of the women who paid their own fines paid for a general licence – to marry whomsoever they pleased (Bennett, 1981).

On a few manors a young woman, even if she had brothers, was able to acquire and hold land independently before her marriage. This land might be a gift from her father, or she could purchase it with cash accumulated from her work as a servant or wage-labourer, or as an ale-brewer. Although adolescent girls were proportionally less active in the land market than their brothers – at Brigstock only one daughter conveyed and received land for every four sons who did so – these women did enjoy full legal autonomy over their lands. They were free to dispose of them as they wished: they personally answered for criminal actions and offences such as trespass and, as tenants, they were legally required to render suit to court. They thus enjoyed a freedom and independence that they would lose as soon as they married (Bennett, 1987: 65–99). In the state of current research it is impossible to say how widespread was this practice of active adolescent female participation in the land market. On many Sussex manors, both before and after the Black Death, the only adolescent women holding land were those who inherited it on the deaths of their parents. Young women neither received land as gifts from living fathers, nor purchased it with their own funds (Mate, 1998). So too on the manor of Hevingham in north-east Norfolk, women rarely held land independently before widowhood in the late fifteenth and sixteenth centuries. Whittle attributed this to a preference for giving daughters cash rather than land as their share of the family inheritance (Whittle, 1998). That is surely part of the explanation. Over the course of the fourteenth century in much of England it became as common among customary tenants as among freeholders to give daughters a marriage portion in money and/or goods instead of a dowry in land. Yet in line with the Brigstock experience, some young women should have been able to purchase land. That they did not suggests that opportunities for female employment were limited in both Sussex and north-east Norfolk.

Within the towns, land held under the form of property law known as burgage tenure could often be freely divided. A merchant could give town houses to daughters, even if he had sons, or to a sister instead of a brother. In addition, in some boroughs such as Exeter partible inheritance gave daughters equal shares with their brothers in the parental property. These enhanced inheritance opportunities led Kowaleski to suggest that women played critical roles in the formation and descent of urban properties and businesses (Kowaleski, 1988: 49). In mid-fifteenth-century Bury St Edmunds, Emma Goldsmith, 'single woman', was one of the city's most prominent rentiers (Gottfried, 1982: 149). Yet opportunities were not always realized. At Exeter, for example, although a woman could practise a trade on her own, or use her inheritance to benefit her own enterprise, Kowaleski found that more often than not she practised a trade, or continued to practise a trade that her husband had initiated and her inheritance benefited her husband's economic position more than her own (Kowaleski, 1986: 146). Fathers, even when they could will property to daughters, preferred to give them cash marriage portions. The urban property of married women, like land in the countryside, would be managed and controlled by their husbands, and could be, and often was, alienated during the women's lifetime, albeit with their consent. Although unmarried daughters could become rentiers, like Emma Goldsmith, or run a business on their own, such action was discouraged by the prevailing belief that a woman's *primary* career was that of wife and mother and that the demands of her husband's business should take precedence over her own wishes. Most young urban heiresses, like their rural sisters, married fairly soon after receiving their inheritance, and were content to adapt their working lives to their husband's needs.

Urban women might also enjoy trading privileges and the right to belong to a guild or fraternity. At London, and certain other towns such as Exeter, a married woman could elect to trade independently as a *femme sole*. She was allowed to train her own apprentices, both men and women, and to be answerable for her own debts. Women also had the right to participate in guild ceremonials such as members' funerals, and to attend some, but not necessarily all, feasts. In general, however, women were treated as second-class guild members. Guild membership, for example, did not give women any right to participate in civic politics. Married women often paid lower admission fees, were barred from wearing guild livery and did not participate in the most important social events. Furthermore, in the vast majority of guilds no women could vote for guild officials, serve as guild officers or take part in guild political or judicial activities (Kowaleski and Bennett, 1989: 11–38). Although there are a few examples of a woman serving on a guild council, or publicly supervising a trade, it seems clear that 'women's particiation in craft guild organization and quality control was exceptional' (Jewell, 1996: 164).

A few women were also admitted to the freedom of some cities and thus enjoyed many of the privileges that belonged with that position. In London the widow of a London citizen could be a free woman in her own right so long as she remained unmarried. This status gave her the right to conduct business independently within the city: she could open a shop and trade retail, she could wage her law in the city courts (i.e., clear herself by producing in court a specified number of oath-helpers) and when she traded outside the city her goods would be privileged in other towns and markets like those of other London citizens (Barron, 1989; Barron and Sutton, 1994: xiii–xxxiv). At Exeter, on the other hand, women, including widows, were generally barred from the franchise. At York, daughters were sometimes admitted by right of redemption or purchase but their numbers were small. Elsewhere, such as Hull and Nottingham, Shrewsbury and Canterbury, women had to purchase a licence to trade.

As a result of the research carried out in the last fifteen years historians now understand more clearly the legal processes at work in both common and customary law. Much less is known about their impact on the lives of women. A man, through the mechanism of enfeoffment to use, could bequeath land to non-inheriting daughters as well as non-inheriting sons. In the early sixteenth century some fathers were leaving property to daughters who wished to remain single, but it is not clear how widespread this practice was nor when it first became common (Mate, 1998). Work on the plea rolls of the central royal courts at Westminster by Walker and Mate and on the court of hustings by Hanawalt have all illustrated that a widow's enjoyment of her dower or jointure was by no means automatic, but that she did have some legal form of redress. In many cases her suit was successful, albeit costly and time-consuming. What is not yet clear is whether the majority of widows benefited or lost from the new procedures that became so popular in the century and a half after 1348. All that can be said at present is that some widows got more and others less than they would have done in similar circumstances in the early Middle Ages. Furthermore widows, at all levels of society, were pressured to accept cash or an annuity instead of taking up their land, but again it is not clear how this affected the lives of the women concerned. Cases brought before the Court of Chancery complaining about annuities being many years in arrears clearly show that some widows were very vulnerable, but not whether the majority were.

The situation regarding the rights of widows and daughters of customary tenants is even more obscure, since each manor had its own set of customs regulating inheritance and the provision made for widows as well as the mechanism under which land was held. Thus in some places in the late fourteenth century widows continued to enjoy their traditional right to a third or a half of their husbands' holdings as their dower. Elsewhere a husband and wife had joint tenure, or land might be granted in the form of 'three lives' – to a man, his wife and their designated heir. Work already done, however, clearly indicates distinct regional variations. Deathbed transfers, for example, were much more common on the manors studied by Smith than on the Sussex manors studied by Mate. So, too, grants of land to adolescent daughters, so prevalent at Brigstock before the plague, did not occur everywhere. Only more detailed research at the local manorial level will determine how practices changed over time and whether any developments concerning property rights were common to the whole country.

One change that clearly improved women's lives was the new canon law conception of marriage. Unions formed either by the couple's free consent, expressed by exchange of vows in the present tense, or by a promise of future marriage followed by sexual intercourse, were regarded by ecclesiastical courts as legally binding, although clandestine and irregular. No public ceremony, and no parental or seigneurial consent, was necessary. Studies of cases that came before the ecclesiastical courts show that by the fifteenth century people did know that words could make a marriage, but were not always clear what precise form those words should take. Thus ambiguous phrases such as 'it pleases me to have you as my husband' or 'behold my oath that I shall be at your disposal' ultimately formed the basis of litigation about whether or not a marriage had taken place (Helmholz, 1974; Pedersen, 1994). Although most young women would not consent to sexual activity until an agreement of marriage had been made, some couples did live together with the intention of not marrying. Other couples were willing to contract a clandestine marriage which consisted simply of mutual promises before witnesses, without any subsequent public solemnization in the presence of a priest (Sheehan, 1971).

To what extent did young women in late medieval England have freedom of choice over their future spouse? The disappearance of the marriage levy of merchet eliminated the possibility of seigneurial influence over peasants. But in the case of land held by military tenure, where the right to arrange for the marriage of an heir or heiress belonged to the lord, or the person to whom he had sold or assigned the right, a young girl could still be married to someone not of her choosing. The church's teaching, however, did make it easier for her to turn down a prospective spouse for whom she had strong objections. On the other hand, parental influence remained strong. L. R. Poos, in his study of fifteenth-century Essex, has come to the conclusion that couples, while they recognized that they were permitted to enter marriage of their own free will and with little ceremony, still desired to secure the assent of parents and other relatives and friends whenever those parents were still alive and residing in close proximity to the couple (Poos, 1991: 135). Likewise, parents expected to influence their children's choice of partner, but knew that they could not prevent a child from marrying 'of her own minde pleasure'. Fathers, therefore, often insisted in their wills that if a daughter married against the wishes of her mother or legal guardian she would lose part or all of her marriage portion. Thus daughters who remained under the parental roof or who hoped to receive financial support towards their marriage almost certainly had less freedom of choice over their marriage partner than those girls who had left home to work for wages and who were responsible for paying for their own dowries. Once a marriage had been entered into, it could not easily be dissolved. Although the term 'divorce' appears in the records, it did not have its modern meaning, but referred either to a judicial separation or to an annulment, a declaration that a marriage had been invalid from the beginning. A judicial separation was allowed for three causes: adultery, 'spiritual' fornication (heresy or apostasy) and cruelty. The couple was not forced to live together, but neither partner was free to remarry. Both parties could remarry if the marriage was annulled, but an annulment was not easy to achieve. To succeed one had to prove, for example, the man's natural impotence, that the marriage had been entered into under duress or that the partners had been too closely related by blood. By and large people were aware of the church's teaching on marriage and were prepared to conform to it (Helmholz 1974: 74–107). Marriage, especially when carried out with formal public ceremony, could be very expensive. Gifts were frequently exchanged, and guests had to be entertained. This might involve no more than a simple repast of bread and ale, but in the cases of the nobility and the gentry might involve sumptuous feasts over several days. Finally, the young couple needed the means to set up house for themselves. The size of the marriage portion obviously varied from the few marks that was all that an artisan family could afford to the 1,000 marks that was common among the nobility. A young woman who received no financial help from her parents, and who was unable to save much from her earnings might have to delay marriage, or not marry at all because of lack of means.

Conclusion

In looking at this whole time period, there is much about women's lives that we still don't know and there is no picture of steady progress in either women's rights or opportunities. Gains in one place or at one time were matched by losses elsewhere. Exceptional circumstances changed, so did the opportunity. The lack of organization in the church in the early years after the conversion to Christianity, and the need for educational and missionary activity, allowed female members of royal houses, such as Hild, to influence ecclesiastical affairs in ways that subsequent abbesses were never able to regain. Likewise the absence of a centralized, professional bureaucracy in the tenth and eleventh centuries made it possible for able and intelligent queens – both before and after 1066 – to exercise patronage and play a more direct role in political affairs than their successors. Even in the late Middle Ages, when the government was primarily in the hands of male administrators, a weak and incompetent ruler such as Henry VI could thrust his spouse on to centre stage. But as Pauline Stafford has constantly reminded us (Stafford, 1997b) a queen remained a woman and was thus a prisoner to the inexorable shifts in the female life-cycle. A wife became a widow and when she did her power might disappear unless her son was willing to sanction its continuance. The situation of Aelfthryth during the reign of her son Aethelred, and of Emma under Harthacanute, was basically similar to that of Margaret Beaufort during the reign of Henry VII. Their actual power and influence was considerable but it was not exercised in their own right, but because of the delegation of their son.

Throughout the medieval period the ownership of land was a

major source of status, prestige and power. The influence of queens was often supported and underpinned by the estates that they were given. Patrilineal inheritance, however, which favoured sons at the expense of daughters, put most women at a distinct disadvantage. Although the establishment of a woman's right to inherit in the absence of male heirs of the same degree went some way towards redressing the balance, this right could be undercut whenever a donor granted land to a named beneficiary and the *male* heirs of his body. In the late medieval period, according to Simon Payling (Payling, 1992) this tail male entail was the exception rather than the rule, but it remained a potential threat to the female acquisition of land. Furthermore if the heiress was already married at the time she received her inheritance her land was legally taken over and managed by her husband. Only in widowhood did an heiress gain full control over her inheritance.

A widow might also be granted a share of her husband's estates, whether in the form of a morning gift, dower or jointure. In the thirteenth and early fourteenth centuries her right to claim this share (her dower) from freehold land that her husband had held *at any time* during the marriage did give some widows a larger portion of land than they would have enjoyed earlier. By the end of the fifteenth century, however, the practice of granting land to trustees meant that dower was no longer the main avenue by which a widow was provided for. She had to rely on the amount of land in which she had been given joint tenure at the time of her marriage, and whatever other provision was made for her by her husband in his will. She might, if she had been granted one of those 'excessive' jointures so bemoaned by political historians, have received a larger share than a widow would have been entitled to earlier, but in many cases she would have received less. Moreover, widows were frequently persuaded or pressured to give up their land in favour of an annuity. If the latter was paid regularly, a widow could have adequate maintenance, but without the land, with its opportunities for lordship, she exercised much less power.

The church's teaching on the need for assent in a valid marriage meant that after the end of the twelfth century widows could no longer be forced to remarry against their will, and young women could refuse the spouse proposed for them by their guardian or parents. None the less, in practice many women were still pressured to marry men chosen by others, not themselves. The greater the wealth and status of the woman, the less the likelihood that she could exercise any freedom of choice. Thus young, aristocratic girls were married to men ten or more years older than themselves or to men from distant counties whom they scarcely knew. Only a few, independent-minded, aristocratic women actually married according to their 'owne minde pleasure' and withstood the threat of the loss of parental approval and their marriage portion. Such threats, however, had much less impact on women who had left their home to work elsewhere for wages and who could expect to receive little from their parents, in either money or goods, by way of a marriage settlement. Thus, for example, a girl whose father was an agricultural labourer or a craftsman would be much freer than a wealthier woman to choose her own marriage partner, but if she worked in a town with a higher proportion of women than men, she might not receive a proposal at all, and would end her days living on the edge of subsistence.

Class as well as gender influenced women's lives. This shows up most clearly in the position of widows. Noble, gentry and rich urban widows usually received some form of maintenance – either land or an annuity. Even though they might be forced to scale down their lifestyle and their standard of living, they did not face the spectre of destitution. Improvements in diet, housing and clothing from the twelfth century onwards meant that by the end of the fifteenth century such widows generally lived in greater material comfort than their predecessors would have done in the tenth and eleventh centuries. How far down the social scale these improvements spread is still not clear. Some families of wage labourers in the fifteenth century did eat better and live in warmer, drier houses than their forebears had done, but others, facing periods of unemployment during the mid-century recession, clearly did not. The well-being of their widows depended a great deal on whether or not they received any real property. A widow who held jointly with her husband a piece of land or an urban tenement could keep it for life and did not forfeit it if she remarried. She was thus in a stronger position than earlier widows of customary tenants who had been forced to give up their property on remarriage, or in some cases when their sons came of age. But by the end of the fifteenth century many widows among the labouring classes were not receiving any real property at all. Forced to live with family or friends and to depend on what they could earn or irregularly paid annuities, they could end their lives in dire straits.

Yet women could not escape the impact of gender inequities. No woman could become a priest, and no woman, at any level, exercised official, legitimated, authority – as village constable, mayor or alderman or member of Parliament. Women who wanted to lead a formal, religious life could do so only in a cloistered house, and they had fewer and generally poorer institutions to choose from. Moreover, in each social class fewer women than men had access to literacy and education. Furthermore, although after the Black Death more women entered the paid labour force than earlier, they frequently worked fewer days and earned less than their male counterparts. The fact that a few women, usually widows, ran a successful business, such as a bell-foundry, does not alter the situation that the majority of women continued to fill low-paid positions in service, or in the textile and victualling trades. Supervisory positions, even for areas such as dairying that were dominated by women, generally remained in male hands. Finally, work such as child-care, laundry and household management remained very much 'women's work', so that whenever a married woman worked in the fields or in a shop she did so in addition to her other domestic responsibilities.

One might have expected population losses on the magnitude of those occurring after 1348 to have had a more long-lasting effect on the position of women. That they did not stems primarily from the prevailing ideology in which the work and actions of men were valued more highly than the work of women. An heiress who was married used her inheritance to benefit her husband's business, not to establish a trade of her own. Women were content to go into the workforce when there was a demand for them, and to leave when they were no longer needed. They did not develop a work-identity of their own, but identified with the trade of their husbands. So, too, women who exercised patronage found places for men, and queens furthered the careers of their sons, not their daughters. In a hierarchal society in which children were subservient to their parents, and servants to their employers, it was not surprising that so many women accepted the authority of fathers or husbands. A woman who believed that she was weaker than a man, not only physically, but morally and intellectually (less rational) did not question the right of her father to choose her husband and her husband to manage her property.

To sum up: were the Middle Ages, or any part of this time, a golden age for women: did women, as women, make any significant advances? The answer, to my mind, is no. Despite evidence that individual women could exercise considerable economic and political clout, women as a group did not enjoy any kind of legal or economic equality. Examples of working economic partnerships between husbands and wives at various levels of society do not alter the fact that married women were legally subordinate to their husbands. In the period following the Black Death, the expansion in the number of heiresses and the number of female workers in the labour force did not lead to any transformation in women's roles. Although in times of acute labour shortage a few women undertook formerly male tasks, they did not become permanent employees. Occupational segregation, with higher-paid, high-status positions in the hands of men, remained firmly in place. When brewing ceased to be a low-paid, low-status occupation, women lost their place within it. Likewise, although legal changes allowed some women greater access to land, overall, at any time throughout the period, women controlled a smaller percentage of landed resources than men. Yet at no time in the Middle Ages can women be regarded as downtrodden. Prior to marriage, in the absence of their husbands and as widows women successfully managed households, businesses and land. Despite the negative ideology, many women took advantage of the opportunities that society did offer, and were able to lead rich and productive lives.

References

Abram, A., 1916. 'Women Traders in Medieval London', *Economic Journal*, 26, pp. 276–85.

Acheson, Eric, 1992. *A Gentry Community: Leicestershire in the Fifteenth Century c. 1422–1485* (Cambridge).

Aers, David, 1988. 'The Making of Margery Kempe: Individual and Community' in *Community, Gender and Individual Identity* (London and New York).

Archer, R., 1984. 'Rich Old Ladies: the Problem of Late Medieval Dowagers', in *Property and Politics: Essays in Later Medieval History*, ed. A. Pollard (Gloucester and New York), pp. 15–35.

——— 1992. '"How Ladies ... who live on their manors ought to manage their households and estates": Women as Landholders and Administrators in the Later Middle Ages', in *Woman is a Worthy Wight*, ed. P. J. P. Goldberg (Stroud, Glos.)

Armstrong, C. A. J., 1942. 'The Piety of Cicely, Duchess of York: A Study in Late Medieval Culture', in *For Hilaire Belloc: Essays in Honor of His 71st Birthday*, ed. Douglas Woodruff (New York).

Aston, Margaret, 1980. 'Lollard Women Priests?', *Journal of Ecclesiastical History*, xxxi, pp. 441 61.

Atkinson, Clarissa, 1983. *Mystic and Pilgrim: The Book and the World of Margery Kempe* (Ithaca and London).

Ault, Warren O., 1972. *Open-Field Farming in Medieval England* (London).

Bailey, Mark, 1996. 'Demographic Decline in Late Medieval England: Some Thoughts on Recent Research', *Economic History Review*, 2nd ser., xlix, pp. 1–19.

Bardsley, S., 'Women's Work Reconsidered. Gender and Wage Differentiation in Late Medieval England' *Past and Present* (forthcoming).

Barron, C., 1985. 'The Parish Fraternities of Medieval London', in *The Church in Pre-Reformation Society*, ed. C. Barron and C. Harper-Bill (Woodbridge), pp. 13–37.

1989. 'The Golden Age of Women in Medieval London', *Reading Medieval Studies*, xv (1989), pp. 35–58.

1994. 'Johanna Hill (*d.* 1441) and Johanna Sturdy (*d.* 1460) Bellfounders', in *Medieval London Widows*, ed. Barron and Sutton, pp. 99–111.

1996. 'The Education and Training of Girls in Fifteenth Century London', in *Courts, Counties and the Capital in the Later Middle Ages*, ed. Diane E. S. Dunn (Stroud/New York), pp. 139–53.

Barron, C. and Sutton A., eds. 1994. *Medieval London Widows 1300–1500* (London).

Bateson, M., 1899. *Records of the Borough of Leicester, 1103–1327* (London).

Beckwith, Sarah, 1992. 'The Problems of Authority in Late Medieval English Mysticism: Language, Agency and Authority in the Book of Margery Kempe', *Exemplaria*, 4, pp. 171–99.

Bell, Susan Groag, 1982. 'Medieval Women Book Owners: Arbiters of Lay Piety and Ambassadors of Culture', *Signs*, 7, reprinted in *Women and Power in the Middle Ages*, ed. Erler and Kowaleski (Athens, Georgia, 1988) and in *Sisters and Workers in the Middle Ages*, ed. J. M. Bennett (Chicago, 1989).

Bennett, H. S., 1932. *The Pastons and Their England*, 2nd edn. (Cambridge).

Bennett. J., 1981. 'Medieval Peasant Marriage: An Examination of Marriage License Fines in *Liber Gersumarum*', in *Pathways to Medieval Peasants*, ed. J. A. Raftis (Toronto), pp. 193–246.

1986. 'The Village Ale-wife: Women and Brewing in Fourteenth Century England', in *Women and Work in Pre-industrial Europe*, ed. B. A. Hanawalt (Bloomington, Indiana), pp. 20–36.

1987. *Women in the Medieval English Countryside: Gender and Household in Brigstock before the Plague* (New York and Oxford).

1988. 'Public Power and Authority in the Medieval English Countryside', in *Women and Power in the Middle Ages*, ed. Erler and Kowaleski (Athens, Georgia).

1992a. 'Medieval Women, Modern Women: Across the Great Divide', in *Culture and History, 1350–1600*, ed. David Aers (London), pp. 147–75.

1992b. 'Widows in the Medieval English Countryside', in *Upon my Husband's Death*, ed. Louise Mirrer (Ann Arbor), pp. 69–114.

1996. *Ale, Beer and Brewsters in England: Women's Work in a Changing World 1300–1600* (New York and Oxford).

Bideau, A., 1980. 'A Demographic and Social Analysis of Widowhood and Remarriage', *Journal of Family History*, V, pp. 28–43.

Bonfield, L. and Poos, L. R., 1988. 'The Development of the Deathbed Transfer in Medieval English Manor Courts', *Cambridge Law*

Journal, 47, pp. 403–27, reprinted in *Medieval Society and the Manor Court*, ed. Z. Razi and R. Smith (Oxford, 1996).

Brand, P. and Hyams, P. R., 1983. 'Seigneurial Control of Women's Marriage', *Past and Present*, 99, pp. 122–33.

Britnell, R., 1986. *Growth and Decline in Colchester 1300–1525* (Cambridge).

Brown, E. A. R., 1976. 'Eleanor of Aquitaine: Parent, Queen, and Duchess', in *Eleanor of Aquitaine, Patron and Politician*, ed. W. W. Kibler (Austin and London).

Buckstaff, F. G., 1883. 'Married Women's Property in Anglo-Saxon and Anglo-Norman Law and the Origin of Common Law Dower', *Annals of the American Academy of Political and Social Science*, IV, 233–64.

Carlin, M., 1996. *Medieval Southwark* (London).

Carpenter, Christine, 1992. *Locality and Politics: A Study of Warwickshire Landed Society 1401–1499* (Cambridge).

Chibnall, Marjorie, 1951. *Select Documents of English Lands of the Abbey of Bec*, Camden, third ser., vol. Lxxiii (London).

1991. *The Empress Matilda* (Oxford).

Clark, E., 1987. 'The Decision to Marry in Thirteenth and Early Fourteenth Century Norfolk', *Mediaeval Studies*, 49, pp. 496–516.

1996. 'Charitable Bequests, Deathbed Land Sales and the Manor Court in Later Medieval England', in *Medieval Society and the Manor Court*, ed. Z. Razi and R. Smith (Oxford), pp. 143–61.

Cross, Claire, 1978. 'Great Reasoners in Scripture: the Activities of Women Lollards, 1380–1530', in *Medieval Women*, ed. Derek Baker, pp. 359–80.

Cullum, R. H., 1992. '"And her Name was Charite." Charitable Giving by and for Women in Late Medieval Yorkshire', in *Woman is a Worthy Wight*, ed. P. J. P. Goldberg (Stroud), pp. 182–211.

Dale, Marion K., 1933. 'The London Silkwomen of the Fifteenth Century', *Economic History Review*, iv, pp. 324–35.

Davies, Matthew, 1994. 'Thomasyne Percyvale, "The Maid of Week" (d. 1312)' in *Medieval London Widows*, ed. C. M. Barron and Anne Sutton (London), pp. 185–208.

Delaney, Sheila, 1975. 'Sexual Economics, Chaucer's Wife of Bath and the *Book of Margery Kempe*', *the minnesota review*, 5, pp. 104–15.

Dickman, Susan, 1984. 'Margery Kempe and the Continental Tradition of the Pious Woman', in the *Medieval Mystical Tradition in England*, ed. Marion Glasscoe (Cambridge, and Woodbridge, Suffolk), pp. 150–68.

Dietrich, Sheila C., 1979. 'An Introduction to Women in Anglo-Saxon Society', in *The Women of England*, ed. Barbara Kanner (Hamden, Connecticut), pp. 32–56.

Dinn, Diana, 1995. 'Margaret of Anjou, Queen Consort of Henry VI; A

Reassessment of Her Role, 1445–53', in *Crown, Government and People in the Fifteenth Century*, ed. Rowena E. Archer (New York), pp. 107–43.

Donahue, Charles Jnr., 1993. 'Female Plaintiffs in Marriage Cases in the Court of York in the Later Middle Ages: What Can We Learn from the Numbers?', in *Wife and Widow in Medieval England*, ed. S. S. Walker, pp. 188–218.

Duffy, Eamon, 1990. 'Holy Maydens, Holy Wyfes: the Cult of Women Saints in Fifteenth- and Sixteenth-Century England', in *Women in the Church*, ed. W. J. Sheils and D. Wood (published for the Ecclesiastical History Society, Oxford), pp. 175–96.

1992. *The Stripping of the Altars* (New Haven and London).

Dyer, C. C., 1979. *Lords and Peasants in a Changing Society: The Estates of the Bishopric of Worcester 680–1540* (Cambridge).

Elkins, S., 1988. *Holy Women in Twelfth Century England* (Chapel Hill).

Faith, R. J., 1983. 'Seigneurial Control of Women's Marriage', *Past and Present*, 99, pp. 133–48.

Fell, Christine, 1984. *Women in Anglo-Saxon England and the Impact of 1066* (Bloomington, Indiana).

1990. 'Some Implications of the Boniface Correspondence', in *New Readings on Women in Old English Literature*, ed. H. Damico and A. Hennessey Olson (Bloomington, Indiana).

Franklin, Peter, 1986. 'Peasant Widows "Liberation" and Remarriage before the Black Death', *Economic History Review*, 2nd. ser., xxxix, pp. 186–204.

Gates, L., 1996, 'Widows, Property, and Remarriage: Lessons from Glastonbury's Deverill Manors', *Albion*, 28, pp. 19–35.

Gilchrist, Roberta, 1994. *Gender and Material Culture: The Archaeology of Religious Women* (London and New York).

Gilchrist, R. and Marilyn Oliva, 1993. *Religious Women in Medieval East Anglia: Studies in East Anglian History, I* (Norwich).

Goldberg, P. J. P., 1986. 'Female Labor, Service and Marriage in the Late Medieval Urban North', *Northern History*, 22, pp. 18–38.

1988. 'Women in Fifteenth Century Town Life', in *Towns, Townspeople and the Fifteenth Century*, ed. J. A. F. Thomson (Gloucester).

1991. 'The Public and the Private: Women in the Pre-Plague Economy', in *Thirteenth Century England, III*, ed. P. R. Coss and S. D. Lloyd (Woodbridge, Suffolk).

1992a. *Women, Work and Life Cycle in a Medieval Economy: York and Yorkshire c. 1300–1520* (Oxford).

1992b. *Woman is a Worthy Wight* (Stroud).

Gottfried, Robert S., 1982. *Bury St. Edmunds and The Urban Crisis: 1290–1539* (Princeton, New Jersey).

Graham, H., 1992. ' "A Woman's Work ...".: Labor and Gender in the

Late Medieval Countryside', in *Woman is a Worthy Wight*, ed. P. J. P. Goldberg (Stroud).

Gross, Charles, 1890. *The Gild Merchant*, 2 vols., reprinted 1927, 1964 (Oxford).

Hale, William Hale, 1865. *Registrum sive Liber Irrotularius et Consuetudinarius Prioratus Beatae Mariae Wigorniensis*, Camden Soc., vol. xci (London).

Halpin, P., 1994. 'Women Religious in Late Anglo-Saxon England', *The Haskins Society Journal*, vol. vi, pp. 97–110.

Hanawalt, B. A., 1986a. *The Ties That Bound: Peasant Families in Medieval England* (New York).

1986b. 'Peasant Women's Contribution to the Home Economy in Late Medieval England', in *Women and Work in Pre-Industrial England*, ed. B. A. Hanawalt (Bloomington, Indiana), pp. 3–19.

1988. 'Lady Honor Lisle's Networks of Influence', in *Women and Power in the Middle Ages*, ed. M. Erler and M. Kowaleski (Athens, Georgia), pp. 188–213.

1992. 'The Widow's Mite: Recovery of Dower in Late Medieval London', in *Upon My Husband's Death: Widows in the Literature and History of Medieval Europe*, ed. Louise Mirrer (Ann Arbor), pp. 21–45.

1993. 'Remarriage as an Option for Urban and Rural Widows in Late Medieval England', in *Wife and Widow: The Experiences of Women in Medieval England* (Ann Arbor), pp. 141–63.

1995. 'At the Margins of Women's Space in Medieval Europe', in *Matrons and Marginal Women in Medieval Society*, ed. R. R. Edwards and V. Ziegler (Woodbridge, Suffolk), pp. 1–17.

Harris, B., 1990a. 'Women and Politics in Early Tudor England', *Historical Journal*, 33, 259–81.

1990b. 'Property, Power and Personal Relations: Elite Mothers and Sons in Yorkist and Early Tudor England', *Signs*, 15, pp. 606–32.

Harvey B., 1976. *Westminster Abbey and Its Estates in the Middle Ages* (Oxford).

Harvey, P. D. A., ed. 1976. *Manorial Records of Cuxham, Oxfordshire* (London).

Haskell, Ann S., 1973. 'The Paston Women on Marriage in Fifteenth Century England', *Viator*, 4, pp. 459–71.

Helmholz, R. H., 1974. *Marriage Litigation in Medieval England* (Cambridge).

Hilton, R., 1975. *The English Peasantry in the Later Middle Ages* (Oxford).

Hollis, Stephanie, 1992. *Anglo-Saxon Women and the Church: Sharing a Common Fate* (Woodbridge, Suffolk).

Holt, J. C., 1965. *Magna Carta* (Cambridge).

1985. 'Feudal Society and the Family in Early Medieval England: IV

The Heiress and the Alien', *Transactions of the Royal Historical Society*, ser. 5, xxxv, pp. 1–28.

Honeycott, Lois L., 1995. 'Intercession and the High Medieval Queen: the Esther Topos', in *The Power of the Weak*, ed. J. Carpenter and S. MacLean (Urbana and Chicago), pp. 126–46.

Howell, Cecily, 1983. *Land, Family and Inheritance in Transition: Kibworth Harcourt, 1280–1700* (Cambridge).

Hutton, D., 1985. 'Women in Fourteenth Century Shrewsbury', in *Women and Work in Pre-Industrial England*, ed. L. Charles and L. Duffin (London), pp. 83–99.

Hyams, Paul R., 1980. *Kings, Lords and Peasants in Medieval England: The Common Law of Villeinage in the Twelfth and Thirteenth Centuries* (Oxford).

Jesch, J., 1991. *Women in the Viking Age* (Woodbridge, Suffolk).

Jewell, Helen, 1996. *Women in Medieval England* (Manchester and New York).

Jones, Michael K. and Malcolm G. Underwood, 1992. *The King's Mother: Lady Margaret Beaufort, Countess of Richmond and Derby* (Cambridge).

Karras, Ruth Mazo, 1989. 'The Regulation of Brothels in Later Medieval England', *Signs*, 14, pp. 399–433.

1996. *Common Women: Prostitution and Sexuality in Medieval England* (Oxford and New York).

Keene, D., 1985. *Survey of Medieval Winchester*, 2 vols. (Oxford).

1994. 'Tanners' Widows, 1300–1350', in *Medieval London Widows*, ed. Barron and Sutton, pp. 1–27.

Kettle, Ann J. 1995. 'Ruined Maids: Prostitutes and Servant Girls in Later Medieval England', in *Matrons and Marginal Women*, ed. R. R. Edwards and V. Ziegler (Woodbridge, Suffolk), pp. 19–31.

Klapisch-Zuber, C., 1985. *Women, Family and Ritual in Renaissance Italy* (Chicago).

Klinck, Anne L., 1982. 'Anglo-Saxon Women and the Law', *Journal of Medieval History*, 8, pp. 107–21.

Kowaleski, M., 1986. 'Women's Work in a Market Town, Exeter in the Late Fourteenth Century', in *Women and Work in Pre-industrial England*, ed. B. Hanawalt, pp. 145–64.

1988. 'The History of Urban Families in Medieval England', *Journal of Medieval History*, 14, pp. 47–63.

1995. *Local Markets and Regional Trade in Medieval Exeter* (Cambridge).

Kowaleski, M. and J. Bennett, 1989. 'Crafts, Gilds, and Women in the Middle Ages: Fifty Years after Marian K. Dale', in *Sisters and Workers in the Middle Ages*, ed. J. M. Bennett *et al.* (Chicago and London), pp. 11–38.

Lacey, K., 1985. 'Women and Work in Fourteenth and Fifteenth Century

London', in *Women and Work in Pre-Industrial England*, ed. L. Charles and L. Duffin (London), pp. 24–82.

Laughton, J., 1995. 'The Alewives of Later Medieval Chester', in *Crown, Government and People in the Fifteenth Century*, ed Rowena A. Archer (New York), pp. 191–208.

Lazar, Moshe, 1976. 'Cupid, the Lady, and the Poet: Modes of Love at Eleanor of Aquitaine's Court', in *Eleanor of Aquitaine: Patron and Politician*, ed. William W. Kibler (Austin and London), pp. 35–59.

Lees, Clare A. and Overing, Gillian R., 1994. 'Birthing Bishops and Fathering Poets; Bede, Hild, and the Relations of Cultural Production', *Exemplaria*, pp. 35–65.

Leyser, Henrietta, 1995. *Medieval Women: A Social History of Women in England* (London).

Lochrie, Karma, 1986. 'The Book of *Margery Kempe*: the Marginal Woman's Quest for Literary Authority', *Journal of Medieval and Renaissance Studies*, 16, pp. 33–55.

Loengard, Janet Senderowitz, 1985. 'Of the Gift of Her Husband: English Dower and Its Consequences in the year 1200', in *Women of the Medieval World*, ed. J. Kirshner and S. Wemple (Oxford), pp. 215–55.

1993. 'Rationalis Dos: Magna Carta and the Widow's "Fair Share" in the Earlier Thirteenth Century', in *Wife and Widow in Medieval England*, ed. Sue Sheridan Walker (Ann Arbor), pp. 59–80.

McIntosh, M. K., 1986. *Autonomy and Community: The Royal Manor of Havering, 1200–1500* (Cambridge).

McNamara, J., 1994. 'The *Herrenfrage*: Restructuring the Gender System, 1050–1150', in *Medieval Masculinities*, ed. C. A. Lees (Minneapolis and London), pp. 3–30.

McSheffrey, Shannon, 1995. *Gender and Heresy: Women and Men in Lollard Communities* (Philadelphia).

Maddern, P., 1988. 'Honor Among the Pastons: Gender and Integrity in Fifteenth Century English Provincial Life', *Journal of Medieval History*, 14, pp. 357–71.

Mate, M. 1991. 'The Agrarian Economy of South-East England before the Black Death: Depressed or Buoyant', in *Before the Black Death*, ed. Bruce M. S. Campbell (Manchester and New York).

1998. *Daughters Wives and Widows after the Black Death: Women in Sussex, 1350–1530* (Woodbridge, Suffolk).

Mathew, Gervase, 1968. *The Court of Richard II* (London).

Meale, Carol M., ed., 1993. '"Alle the bokes that I have of latyn, englisch, and frensch": Laywomen and Their Books in Late Medieval England', in *Women and Literature in Britain, 1150–1500* (Cambridge).

Meyer, M. A., 1977. 'Women and Tenth Century English Monastic Reform', *Revue Benedictine*, 87, pp. 34–61.

1979. 'Land Charters and the Legal Position of Anglo-Saxon Women', in *The Women of Medieval England*, ed. Barbara Kanner (Hamden, Conn.), pp. 57–82.

1991. 'Women's Estates in Later Anglo-Saxon England: The Politics of Possession', *Haskins Society Journal*, III.

Middleton, C., 1979. 'The Sexual Division of Labor in Feudal England', *New Left Review*, pp. 147–68.

Milsom, S. F. C., 1981. 'Inheritance by Women in the Twelfth and Thirteenth Centuries', in *On the Laws and Customs of England: Essays in Honor of S. E. Thorne*, eds. M. S. Arnold *et al.* (Chapel Hill), pp. 60–89.

Moore, John S., 1989. 'Domesday Slavery', *Anglo-Norman Studies*, xi, ed. R. Allen Brown (Woodbridge, Suffolk).

Moran, Jo Anne Hoeppner, 1985. *The Growth of English Schooling 1340–1548* (Princeton).

Nicholson, Joan, 1978. '*Feminae Gloriosae:* Women in the Age of Bede', in *Medieval Women*, ed. Derek Baker (Oxford), pp. 15–29.

Orme, N., 1984. *From Childhood to Chivalry: The Education of English Kings and Aristocracy, 1066–1530* (London and New York).

Parsons, John Carmi, 1995a. 'The Queen's Intercession in Thirteenth Century England', in *Power of the Weak*, ed. J. Carpenter and S. MacLean (Urbana and Chicago), pp. 147–77.

1995b. *Eleanor of Castille: Queen and Society in Thirteenth Century England* (New York).

Partner, Nancy, 1991. 'Reading the *Book of Margery Kempe*', *Exemplaria*, 3, pp. 29–66.

Payling, S. J., 1991. *Political Society in Lancastrian England: The Greater Gentry of Nottinghamshire* (Oxford).

1992. 'Social Mobility, Demographic Change and Landed Society in Late Medieval England', *Economic History Review*, 2nd ser., 45, pp. 51–73.

1995. 'The Politics of Family: Late Medieval Marriage Contracts', in *The McFarlane Legacy*, ed. R. H. Britnell and A. J. Pollard (Stroud and New York).

Pedersen, Frederik, 1994. 'Did the Medieval Laity Know the Common Law Rules on Marriage? Some Evidence From Fourteenth-Century York Cause Papers', *Medieval Studies*, 56, pp. 111–52.

Pelteret, David, 1995. *Slavery in Early Medieval England* (Woodbridge, Suffolk).

Penn, Simon A. C., 1987. 'Female Wage-earners in Late Fourteenth Century England', *Agricultural History Review*, 35, pp. 1–14.

Phythian-Adams, Charles, 1972. 'Ceremony and the Citizen: The Communal Year at Coventry, 1450–1550', in *Crisis and Order in English Towns*, ed. P. Clark and P. Slack (London).

1979. *Desolation of a City: Coventry and the Urban Crisis of the Late Middle Ages* (Cambridge).

Poos, L. R., 1991. *A Rural Society After the Black Death: Essex 1350–1525* (Cambridge).

Power, E., 1922. *Medieval English Nunneries* (Cambridge).

1924. *Medieval People* (London).

1981. *Medieval Women* (Cambridge).

Ravensdale, J., 1984. 'Population Changes and the Transfer of Customary Land on a Cambridgeshire Manor in the Fourteenth Century', in *Land, Kinship and Life Cycle*, ed. R. M. Smith (Cambridge), pp. 197–225.

Rawcliffe, Carole, 1994. 'Margaret Stodeye, Lady Philipot d. 1431' in *Medieval London Widows*, ed. Barron and Sutton, pp. 85–98.

Razi, Z., 1980. *Life, Marriage and Death in a Medieval Parish: Economy, Society and Demography in Halesowen, 1270–1400* (Cambridge).

1981. 'Family, Land, and the Village Community in Later Medieval England', *Past and Present* 93, pp. 3–36.

1996. 'The Use of Manorial Court Rolls in Demographic Analysis: A Reconsideration', in *Medieval Society and the Manor Court*, ed. Z. Razi and R. Smith (Oxford), pp. 324–34.

Reynolds, Susan, 1994. *Fiefs and Vassals* (Oxford).

Richmond, C., 1985. 'The Pastons Revisited: Marriage and Family in Fifteenth Century England', *Bulletin of the Institute of Historical Research*, 58, 25–36.

Rosenthal, J., 1991. *Patriarchy and Families of Privilege in Fifteenth Century England* (Philadelphia).

Rosser, Gervase, 1984. 'The Essence of Medieval Urban Communities: the Vill of Westminster, 1200–1540', *Transactions of the Royal Historical Society*, 34, reprinted in *The Medieval Town*, ed. R. Holt and G. Rosser (1990).

1989. *Medieval Westminster, 1200–1540* (Oxford).

1994. 'Going to the Fraternity Feast: Commensality and Social Relations in Late Medieval England', *Journal of British Studies*, 33.

Rubin, Miri, 1991. *Corpus Christi: The Eucharist in Late Medieval Culture* (Cambridge).

Scammell, Jean, 1974. 'Freedom and Marriage in Medieval England', *Economic History Review*, 2nd ser., xxvii, pp. 523–37.

1976. 'Wife-rents and Merchet', *Economic History Review*, 2nd ser., xxix, pp. 487–90.

Schulenburg, Jane Tibbetts, 1989. 'Women's Monastic Communities, 500–1100', in *Signs* 14, reprinted in *Sisters and Workers in the Middle Ages*, ed. J. M. Bennett *et al.* (Chicago), pp. 208–39.

Searle, Eleanor, 1976. 'Freedom and Marriage in Medieval England: An

Alternative Hypothesis', *Economic History Review*, 2nd ser., xxix, pp. 482–6.

1979. 'Seigneurial Control of Women's Marriage: the Antecedents and Function of Merchet in England', *Past and Present*, lxxxii, pp. 3–43.

Sheehan, M. M., 1971. 'The Formation and Stability of Marriage in Fourteenth Century England: Evidence of an Ely Register', *Medieval Studies*, 33, pp. 228–63.

Smith, R. M., 1983. 'Some Thoughts on "Hereditary" and "Proprietary" Rights under Customary Law in Thirteenth and Early Fourteenth Century England', *Law and History Review*, 1, pp. 95–128.

1984. 'Some Issues Concerning Families and Their Property in Rural England, 1250–1800', in *Land, Kinship and Life Cycle*, ed. R. M. Smith (Cambridge).

1986. 'Women's Property Rights under Customary Law: Some Developments in the Thirteenth and Fourteenth Centuries', *Transactions of the Royal Historical Society*, 5th ser., 26, pp. 165–94.

1991. 'Coping with Uncertainty: Women's Tenure of Customary Land in England 1370–1430', in *Enterprise and Individuals in Fifteenth Century England*, ed. J. Kermode (Stroud, Gloucstershire), pp. 3–67.

1992. 'Geographical Diversity in the Resort to Marriage in Late Medieval Europe: Work, Reputation and Unmarried Females in the Household Formation Systems of Northern and Southern Europe', in *Woman is a Worthy Wight*, ed. P. J. P. Goldberg (Stroud), pp. 16–59.

Spring, E. 1993. *Law, Land and Family* (Chapel Hill and London).

Stafford, Pauline, 1978. 'Sons and Mothers: Family Politics in the Early Middle Ages', in *Medieval Women*, ed. Derek Baker (Oxford), pp. 79–100.

1982. 'The Laws of Cnut and the History of Anglo-Saxon Royal Promises', in *Anglo-Saxon England*, vol. 10, ed. P. Clemoes (Cambridge).

1983. *Queens, Concubines and Dowagers: The King's Wife in the Early Middle Ages* (Athens, Georgia).

1989. *Unification and Conquest: A Political and Social History of England in the Tenth and Eleventh Centuries* (London and New York).

1989. 'Women in Domesday', *Reading Medieval Studies*, 15, pp. 75–94.

1993. 'Kinship and Women in the World of *Maldon*: Byrhtnoth and his Family', in *The Battle of Maldon: Fiction and Fact*, ed. J. Cooper (London).

1994. 'Women and the Norman Conquest', *Transactions of the Royal Historical Society*, sixth ser., 4, pp. 221–49.

1997a. 'Emma: The Powers of the Queen in the Eleventh Century', in *Queens, and Queenship in Medieval Europe*, ed. A. Duggan (Woodbridge, Suffolk), pp. 3–26.

1997b. *Queen Emma and Queen Edith: Queenship and Women's Power in Eleventh Century England* (Blackwell, Oxford).

Stenton, Doris Mary, 1957. *The English Woman in History* (London).

Sutton, A., 1994. 'Alice Claver, Silkwoman (d. 1489)', in *Medieval London Widows*, ed. Barron and Sutton, pp. 129–42.

Swanson, Heather, 1989. *Medieval Artisans* (Oxford).

Tanner, Norman P., 1984. *The Church in Late Medieval Norwich* (Toronto, Pontifical Institute).

Titow, J. Z., 1962. 'Some Differences Between Manors and Their Effects on the Condition of the Peasant in the Thirteenth Century', *Agricultural History Review*, 10, pp. 1–13.

Veale, E., 1994. 'Matilda Penne, Skinner (d. 1392/3)', in *Medieval London Widows*, ed. Barron and Sutton, pp. 47–54.

Walker, Sue Sheridan, 1982. 'Free Consent and the Marriage of Feudal Wards in Medieval England', *Journal of Medieval History*, 8, pp. 123–34.

1993. 'Litigation as a Personal Quest: Suing for Dower in the Royal Courts circa 1272–1350', in *Wife and Widow in Medieval England*, ed. S. S. Walker (Ann Arbor), pp. 81–108.

Ward, J., 1992. *English Noblewomen in the Later Middle Ages* (London).

1994. 'Elizabeth de Burgh, Lady of Clare (d. 1360)' in *Medieval London Widows*, ed. Barron and Sutton, pp. 29–45.

1995. *Women of the English Nobility and Gentry* (Manchester).

Watson, Nicholas, 1993. 'The Composition of Julian of Norwich's *Revelation of Love*', *Speculum*, 68, pp. 637–83.

Waugh, S. L., 1990. 'Women's Inheritance and the Growth of Bureaucratic Monarchy in Twelfth and Thirteenth Century England', *Nottingham Medieval Studies*, xxxiv, pp. 71–92.

Whittle J., 1998. 'Inheritance, Marriage, Widowhood and Remarriage: a Comparative Perspective on Women and Landholding in North-East Norfolk, England, 1440–1580', *Continuity and Change*, vol. 13.

Yorke, Barbara, 1989. 'Sisters Under the Skin, Anglo-Saxon Nuns and Nunneries in Southern England', *Reading Medieval Studies*, xv, pp. 95–117.

Zell, Michael, 1994. *Industry in the Countryside* (Cambridge).

Index

New Studies in Economic and Social History

Titles in the series available from Cambridge University Press

Economic History Society

The Economic History Society, which numbers around 3,000 members, publishes the *Economic History Review* four times a year (free to members) and holds an annual conference.

Enquiries about membership should be addressed to

The Assistant Secretary
Economic History Society
PO Box 70
Kingswood
Bristol
BS15 5TB

Full-time students may join at special rates.